Unfinished

A GUIDE TO DREAM, COMPLETE, AND REPEAT YOUR LIFE'S WORK

Jason Smithers

5ᵗʰ Corner Media LLC.

Maumee, Ohio

Jason Smithers/5th Corner Media LLC.

www.unfinished.life

Book Layout ©2015 BookDesignTemplates.com

Ordering Information:

Quantity sales. Special discounts are available on quantity purchases by corporations, associations, and others. For details, contact:

info@unfinished.life

Unfinished/ Jason Smithers. —1st ed.

ISBN 978-0-9915030-4-9

Contents

i

For my amazing wife Jessica, who always tells me to "go for it."

I love you.

"Remind me that I need to put an inspirational quote here. It would be embarrassing to just have this."

-Jason Smithers

INTRODUCTION

REGRETS

Torschlusspanik *(GERMAN)*

*"The fear that time is running out to act, often
regarding a life goal or opportunity."*[1]

I WANT YOU TO DO SOMETHING. Take your index
finger and touch the space between your eyebrows. You
know, the area you *definitely* don't shave because you were
born with impeccable features and not the singular eyebrow
of the Geico cavemen. An inch or so behind this spot is your
medial orbitofrontal cortex[2]. This area of the brain, no larger
than a marble, is where something very dark lies. An emotion
emanates from that spot that has crippled just about all of us,
driving many to become a shell of who they once were, and is
all but impossible to erase.

Regret.

Regret is that overwhelming feeling of sadness or disappointment over something that has happened. However, regret also consumes us over things that didn't happen, potentially beautiful moments that we've surrendered to fear in exchange for a life married to the "R" word.

When I was sixteen, my friends and I decided to play a game of flashlight tag. Have you ever played? Well, you shouldn't. The object of the game is to hide (at night) while the other kids search for you with their flashlights. You're knighted as "Sir It" if the beam of light hits you. The game is only fun if it's played outdoors in a large area allowing participants to hide and run away from the Mag-Lite's bright beam. This is the perfect game for running around in open backyards and fields, hiding behind trees, and enjoying the mystery of nature. We, however, were in a neighborhood in a not-so-great part of town.

Can you see where this is going? My friend Anthony and I were "it" so we set to the task of finding our friends in the dead of night with just a couple of flashlights. We were pretty sure where they were and didn't want to risk our friends darting away before we could shine our lights on their position. So before we made our move, we decided to duck behind a neighbor's car to prepare for the element of surprise.

"Surprise" was right.

What happened next was a blur. You see, the neighbor whose car we were ducking behind saw us. And to his eyes, we were not kids playing a game! He barreled out of his house towards us — the teenagers he thought were trying to steal the contents of his car.

In a rage he charged at my friend first, who stood tall and tried to reason with the visibly angry, inebriated man.

"We were just playing a ga..."

At that moment, the man was on top of my friend throwing punches left and right.

Still crouched, my right foot had two choices. The first was to push up and try to pull the guy off my friend. The second was to turn the worn sole of my Converse shoe 45 degrees and sprint away.

I had a split second to decide. Just then, another man came out of the house. Decision made! "Run!" My feet heard the command and fled. In that split second decision, I chose to give my medial orbitofrontal cortex plenty of regret to feast on for the next 15 years and counting. I don't remember the run. I don't remember how I found my other friends, who were completely oblivious to the onslaught of punches our friend Anthony was receiving. By the time I explained to them everything that had happened, Anthony was running to us: swollen eyes, blood pouring down his face. He managed to get free and make a break for it.

We eventually had to go to court and testify about what happened that night. Anthony's wounds were treated and would heal, but I know the man who assaulted him wasn't the only one who hurt him that night.

I'm convinced if I would have pushed forward to help Anthony we would have both been pummeled, but I would rather live with getting a few fists to the face than the regret of abandoning my friend.

One motion. One *stupid* turn of the foot. That one decision will live with me forever.

Not everyone's story of regret looks like a game of flashlight tag gone wrong. For many people, it's the things in life that are *good* that we pivot and run from. Instead of working on our dreams, we choose everyday to turn our backs and move in the opposite direction of the book we've always wanted to write, the degree we dreamed of finishing, or the weight we've wanted to lose. Why? Because those things are HARD.

I believe that we love to wax poetic about the things we are going to accomplish in life; but when it comes down to doing the work, we either have no idea where to start, or have no idea how to see it all the way through. With this knowledge, hard goals remain just that: hard. Too hard, in fact. Hard enough that we give up before we put a single bit of energy towards our goals.

About six years ago I decided to get serious about my dreams and goals in life. In these past six years, I've set over 75 goals and hit 45 of them, resulting in 15 races (sprint triathlons, a half marathon, 5ks) completed, a published children's book, three albums that I co-produced, and many other wonderful experiences. None of which I would have been able to finish if I hadn't unpacked what works and what doesn't for me on the journey towards completing these goals.

I don't want you to live with the regret of not completing your goals. I don't want any more negative emotions taking up residence next to your justifiably disappointed feelings towards the series finale of *Lost*. I don't want your medial orbitofrontal cortex to define who you can become.

This book is a collection of the ways I've found to make personal creative goals obtainable for everyone. I want to help you turn the foot forward and meet fear head on. After all, we don't have time to waste on regret. It shouldn't belong in our vocabulary when we are older. Instead, I want to take you from a frustrated individual who has given up trying to complete meaningful, personal work to a person who dreams, completes, and then asks — "Done. What's next?"

CHAPTER 1

Losing Our Meraki

Meraki *(GREEK)*

*"This is a word that modern Greeks often use to describe
doing something with soul, creativity, or love — when
you put "something of yourself" into what you're doing,
whatever it may be. Meraki is often used to describe
cooking or preparing a meal, but it can also mean
arranging a room, choosing decorations, or setting an
elegant table."*[1]

MACI IS OUR OLDER DAUGHTER. SHE'S LIKE A LEAF
that is swept up by the winds of the moment. And wherever
that moment is, she is there, intently focused. When Maci sits
down to draw, she cranks pictures out like a factory worker.
The creative process for her is fluid with no stops. It's almost
as if the crayon is moving her hand and she's just along for
the ride. One day, in a frenzy of creative inspiration, she blew

7

through all of our paper, leaving her with nothing to create on.

Using the impeccable problem-solving skills that every five-year-old comes equipped with, she looked for a flat surface, and found it in the form of my desk. The top of my desk now has a family portrait in marker that will be with us. Forever. And ever. Amen.

Maybe you were once like my daughter. Maybe at an early age, you were told you had an innate knack for creating. Your lines were intentional; every person's features were proportional; your pitch was stellar; your stories were funny; and the process and completion left you full of pride. Above all that, you did it with a sense of MERAKI. Something of yourself was left on the page or canvas, and others could see that.

You couldn't think of anything you would rather do. School couldn't finish fast enough; and when you got home, you'd throw your book bag down in the exact place your mom always told you not to leave it, race to your room, and begin your craft. Completing your works of art never felt tedious. You enjoyed the process of creating just as much as finishing. You weren't fond of revising either, because life hadn't given you any reason to edit. You barely knew what it meant to "start over."

But somewhere along the way, the process became a challenge. "Not good enough yet" crept in by way of a teacher or parent. "This is great, Jamie, but try to soften the face a little. The woman in this picture needs to look less 'manly.'" You began to notice other kids' work as superior to yours.

Some of your peers just seemed naturally more gifted. In your head, you began to compete to either win the favor of these people or be better than them. You lost the drive to put yourself into the work, or maybe you couldn't start a piece without the voices in your head guiding you through the "should" and "should nots" of drawing the human form.

When did this get so hard?

Desire took a back seat to frustration. So you set that part of your life aside. Since you no longer enjoyed the journey and could rarely complete a piece without throwing it away with a hefty helping of self loathing, it was something you could do without. After all, **what's the point** if you can't get on paper what you see in your head? These critical voices cloud your view of the finished product.

Fast-forward a few years. In the garage, you find a folder labeled, "Jamie - 5 years old." You pull out the contents of the folder and in it are all the drawings your parents saved from when you were five. No erase marks, no edits, just the pure joy of creating. Finding these drawings stirs up a lot of emotions within you — both good and bad; a reminder that you were once on a path towards something self-satisfying.

Maybe this isn't your story. Maybe you still would like to create as an adult, but life has thrown the proverbial kitchen sink at you, and the time allotted to make any progress is minimal. You have big goals for your craft, but priorities have shifted. The small amount of free time you have just isn't enough to get yourself into the right frame of mind to create. The desire is there, but it's more like a child pulling on your leg to get you to come play when what is urgent at the moment is paying bills.

The great thing about desire is that it never dies; it's either waiting or hiding, ready to be pulled out of the drawer and into the light the moment you remember the great times creativity brought you, the soul or MERAKI you put into every moment creating.

"The starting point of all achievement is desire"

-Napoleon Hill

Desire can be fickle. It will stay only when it knows it can trust you. It's saying, "I'll stick around and help you, but you have to commit to finish, or I'm leaving." How many adults have you met who have an insatiable desire to keep creating, but no completed work to show for it? I don't know any. The people that show the most passion or MERAKI are the prolific artists that create to completion over and over again.

I've heard it said, "creating art is a *wonderful* journey with no end." I don't know about you, but that sounds awful. If someone told me we were getting in a car and going on a journey with no defined destination, I would question their sanity.

"The end of a melody is not its goal: but nonetheless, had the melody not reached its end it would not have reached its goal either. A parable."

— Friedrich Nietzsche

Every creation has a final form. The natural world around us is full of examples of creation working towards a final form: larva to butterfly, seedling to tree. It's as though creation is on its own mission. It has a will, and my belief is that a Creator wills creation forward.

The final form of human life begins because two human bodies work together to bring forth what started as desire into a physical, living, breathing, laughing, loving, hurting body and soul. A desire, to a zygote, to a fully formed human being. We look at creation's final forms and are inspired by the growth, the process it took to get there; and we celebrate and revere it in all its stages. We capture the process on film; we put it into the rhythm and words of a song.

I believe the desire to create art is pushing us towards *multiple* endings and beginnings, many journeys and destinations within the blip of our short lives. Would Michelangelo have taken the commission to paint the Sistine Chapel if he was told that once he was finished he would have to paint another work of art over his masterpiece, and then one more after that?

No way!

Creators desire the journey, but they want desire to morph into the feeling of satisfaction with the completion of their work. Creating, if done right, is a wonderful journey with many bittersweet endings and exciting beginnings.

This book is meant to be a guide toward the finish line for personal projects, and ultimately a guide towards "Done!" with every project after that, so that one day you can look back at your life's work fulfilled, satisfied with every last screenplay, piece of music, or painting that was ever building up within you. But I believe that to get there, you need to tackle a single project, something you've been kicking around for years — or maybe an idea that just popped in your head that made the hairs stand up on the back of your neck. Discover whatever it is that gives you a sense of purpose, a calling to create and move something from a concept to final form.

IT STARTS WITH ONE

The completion of the first project in front of you, no matter how great or small, is what snowballs the desire to complete bigger and better, over and over. Creating and creativity, art and artistry aren't as difficult as we make these words out to be. We will walk through how to break down large projects into small, simple tasks to check off and give you that momentum to finish.

You have stories to tell, emotions and feelings that need to be displayed in brutal honesty, brushed and stretched out over canvas, songs, words, sounds, and code. But for every story to tell you will have to overcome 10 obstacles to get that story out. That part won't change.

You, like all of creation, are not exempt from the laws of nature. Eggs fall from nests in trees or are devoured by predators, plants wither and die from lack of water's nourishment. Every process of creation has difficulties and enemies to overcome to get to its final form. The elements seem to constantly fight the development process with an unrelenting show of force. Throughout this process you are going to have many obstacles thrown at you to stop you from completing your work.

Even "good" things will stand in the way of completion of something "great." Smartonmoney.com says, "78% of us will have a major negative life event in any given 10 year period of time."[2] Life pulls our focus away from what fulfills us to what we need to do to just survive. My goal isn't going to be to remove the obstacles, but to show you ways to work towards creative fulfillment in the midst of life's toughest obstacles.

Why?

I've been both the teenager that put his art in the drawer out of the feeling of inadequacy *and* the busy husband and father with the staple excuse "I just don't have the time." I wasted 15 years shoving my goals and ideas aside until a tragic life experience reminded me that I'm on this earth for a short time, and I have a responsibility to tell meaningful stories with whatever talents and tools I have at my disposal.

Back in 2008, my wife and I decided we were ready to have children. We had been married for five years and were ready for the joys and up and downs that parenthood would bring. A month into the "creative process" of trying to conceive, we were excited to find out that we would be meeting our first child in less than nine months. We had a routine ultrasound at 20 weeks, only to find that our son had a zero percent chance of survival. We would lose Brayden (we had also found out his gender at the same visit) to a rare genetic disease called anencephaly. Before this, we felt pretty invincible. We were awakened to a harsh reality that our time is fragile, valuable, and fleeting.

We all have a choice in how we will respond to life's toughest realities. Our decision was twofold. One, we would do whatever we could for people who lost a child to this disease that affects 1 in 1000 children. And two, we would live life like we weren't promised another day. Brayden's death changed me in many ways. Before Brayden, I was afraid to share my personal work. I worked as a full-time creative professional for a church, but sharing my *own* creations was something I just didn't do. I grew up as the kid I described in the intro. MERAKI swirled around as I would draw, write stories, or play guitar for hours. But the teenage years and the low self-esteem that came along with them caused me to tuck it all away.

I made a choice not to hide anymore. I would work to be prolific in photography, as well as writing and producing music — and I would do it in spite of life's obstacles or what I personally felt about my art. I know now that I have stories that need to be told to inspire and motivate others, stories I am scared to tell because they have hard truths that are seeping with vulnerability. Stories I think are funny, but I'm worried that others won't get my sense of humor. Stories that need to be shared in the form of whatever medium best conveys my thoughts, because someone out there is going to connect with them. It may be one person or a thousand, but that part is out of my control.

> *"90% completed and shared with the world is better than 100% perfect and tucked away."*[3]
>
> \- *Jon Acuff from Quitter*

My story isn't uncommon. Many people have harder backstories than mine. We all come to the discussion of creativity and can share our past pain, current obstacles, and future hindrances, but those negative circumstances won't win. They won't claim our unfinished work. We'll create in spite of, and through, life's harshest times to share our work with the world. We'll start with your "why?"

Jason Smithers

CHAPTER 2

A Reason for Creating

Ikigai (JAPANESE)

"Ikigai is a Japanese word meaning "reason for being." On the island of Okinawa, it is thought of as "a reason to get up in the morning," a philosophy which has been linked to the longevity of the people there."[1]

I BELIEVE THE LOSS OF OUR SON CREATED SOMETHING IN ME that became the cornerstone of my ability to finish my personal goals and projects. It formed in me the reason "why" I do what I do. It was the soul or Ikigai. Ikigai is why some creations fall flat and others strike a chord in us. I remember when I first heard the band Needtobreathe. Not only did they sound different, but their lyrics were different: full of pain, passion, and the technical musical term

17

"Umph." They had a cause. There was a purpose behind their music. They had a reason to wake up in the morning and create. That resonated with me. Think of your want (desire) and your Ikigai (cause) as two oars on a boat. You need both moving together. If you only have desire, you will spin in circles and never move forward because your purpose hasn't been established. The same goes if you only have Ikigai (cause). You need a passion to motivate you. It doesn't have to be a political movement or the desire to change the world, but it does have to come from the heart. I have many artist friends that create for the purpose of healing. They respond to tragedy or difficult times by building or painting something that can express their feelings better than words.

It's possible you haven't found your "Ikigai" yet. This may have to do with what you are expecting to get out of your work. One effective way to find a cause is to ask yourself, "What moves me to tears or to anger?"

"A gift consists not in what is done or given, but in the intention of the giver or doer."

— *Seneca the Younger, Moral Essays, Volume III: de Beneficiis*

All creations starts as a gift. This is especially true for the ınal. If no one is buying what you've created, essentially sharing your final product with the t being promised anything in return.

If we are honest with ourselves, we expect a transaction to occur with our creative endeavors. Every time I sit down to write a song and it starts to turn into something special, I start to fantasize about the praise I will *receive*. "Man, I should probably call the bomb squad on this track because it's about to BLOW UP." The praise becomes the driving cause, but instead I should be hoping the lyrics connect with someone. I trade good intentions (writing a song to resonate) for bad intentions (praise). This generation has a heightened sense of hidden intentions and can sniff out if your goals for creating are self-serving.

One thing I want to make clear is that we can't accept success and recognition as our Ikigai. That is a byproduct rarely enjoyed by creators, and will only lead to empty pursuits. Studies have shown success and fulfillment rarely go hand in hand. Many of you may have put your craft down because you haven't been blessed to be successful, to be known. There's an encouraging quote in the movie *Basquiat* about the famous Primitivist artist, Jean-Michel Basquiat. It's one line that has stuck with me:

> *"Maybe you aren't famous because your audience hasn't been born yet."*

Your work is your work. Put the notion of success aside and find your good intentions. If pure Ikigai and desire are there, they will find an audience to resonate with. You may not be blessed enough to enjoy having your personal work valued by others in your lifetime, but know that someone, at least one individual, either present or future, will connect with your finished work if the desire and cause are there.

GOOD INTENTIONS OVER BAD

So how do you determine good intentions from bad? Remember, the focus of this book is to help you complete a single dream swirling around in your head.

There's no promise of payment in personal work, so that can't be your driving cause. If I told someone who's never seen my work before that I'm going to create something and I want them to buy it, they are most likely going to pass.

I want you to write down a few responses to the following questions.

1. Who will see or hear my work? Who will be my audience? Who is the recipient of my gift? (Narrow this down.)

2. What emotion do I want people to feel or connect with? What's my theme?

3. How would I feel if only one person connects with it? What if that one person is me?

That last question is the kicker. Upon the completion of your project, you are only promised an audience of one: yourself. How will you feel when you are done? Will the idea of completion be enough to fulfill and carry you through the ~~~~ of ~our project? If so, I'm really happy for you. You've ~oject that gives you joy first and foremost. You've ;ai. But the majority of us would have to be honest and say that if we completed an album, and no one else connected with it, we would be severely disappointed and would probably feel that our time and effort had been wasted.

If the answer to question 3 is "disappointment," then scale the question up. How would you feel if 10 people connect with it? 50 people? 100? 1000? At what number does your disappointment change to excitement?

Personal projects completed with bad intentions will only leave you feeling empty. I can't tell you how many songs, photo compositions, or short videos I've produced with the sole purpose of success, notoriety, relevance, competing with a peer, etc., and every time I reach completion I feel like I cheated the project and myself.

There are major traps that I feel are the top three poor motivators in the pursuit of completing a project.

PAY

It's not inherently bad to pursue compensation for your work. In fact, it can be a great side income, but we need to qualify something here. Remember, the work we are focused on is your personal project. It will have your identity all over it. If someone wants to purchase it for what it is after completion, then that's great; but if the person paying you has a say in the vision of your project from the beginning, then you are no longer working on a personal project. You are freelancing and compromising your vision to meet the buyer's expectations. When we create for others, we are letting them judge our work, which causes our fear and self-doubt to cloud our ability to create.

We need to receive input, feedback, and accountability for completion, but keep other vested interests out of the direction of any personal project.

PRAISE

Praise will only come as a by-product of your work and is never promised by anyone except your mother (Hi, Mom). Expecting massive rounds of praise from your peers and audience upon completion is only a setup for disappointment. People care 1,236 times less about your art than you do (That's a science-y statistic). There's a band I love called Twenty One Pilots. Their music is honest, and I look forward to what they put out. They have been working on a new album. I'm imagining they are losing sleep piecing the songs together, doubting themselves, ripping up lyrics, and starting again. Their process to get to the end product is a battle. Once the album is done, they will promote themselves like crazy and tour in support of the album. I love them and may see a show. I may not. I may tell two friends about their new album; then again, I may not. I may never tweet them to tell them how their lyrics affect me. They may never hear feedback from 80% of the people who listen to their music. And you know what? I believe they'll keep creating, regardless of whether or not I say anything about it because they can't help themselves.

ACCEPTANCE

Acceptance, like praise, is never guaranteed in our personal work. Acceptance can be the antithesis of art when you bend your projects to please others.

"Artists are not cheerleaders, and we're not the heads of tourism boards. We expose and discuss what is problematic, what is contradictory, what is hurtful and what is silenced in the culture we're in."

-Junot Diaz

I'm a people pleaser, and being a people pleaser means that I have specific people in mind I would like to impress with my projects. I subconsciously say to myself:

"Would so-and-so like this part?"

"Will so-and-so think this is cool?"

The final product is a diluted version of what I set out to create. Creating for acceptance will always be a compromise of your art.

WRESTLE TO THE GROUND...

Now comes the hard part. If not for praise, pay or acceptance, then why pursue this project? What will you gain from the amount of hours, self-doubt, and self-loathing your project will produce? It's time to wrestle to the ground the true "why" behind doing ANY personal work from here on out.

Author Mark Murphy has a great book on setting goals titled <u>HARD Goals</u>[2]. His approach states that setting goals should have the following requirements:

• **HEARTFELT** – You have to connect emotionally to your goal. In other words, it has to mean something to you deep down in order to put forth the effort necessary to bring it to life and make it real.

• **ANIMATED** – You also have to have a clear vision of your goal and every aspect of it. You have to be intimately familiar with your goal so that it becomes a living, breathing thing. For instance, if your goal is to buy a house, you have to be able to see your children playing in the yard or visualize your furniture within the home.

• **REQUIRED** – There has to be urgency to your goal, or a desire to act on it immediately. It has to be something that you're not willing to put off until tomorrow, or the next day, or the next.

- **DIFFICULT** – Have you ever heard the notion that if your goal doesn't make you nervous, it isn't big enough? That is more or less the theory behind this particular criterion as your goal must be something that is difficult to do, requiring a bit of effort and commitment on your part.

This is a great start to qualifying your project, but I feel that it needs to be adapted for your desire to dream a bit further. It has to have H.E.A.R.T.

- **HONEST** – Art speaks — and your project should be something you feel you need to say. Boiled-down honesty. It should scare you a bit to say what is on your heart through this project.

- **EVOKING** – All great projects evoke an emotion. Some projects disturb the viewer while others well up nostalgia. For example, one of the emotions I hope to evoke out of the readers of this book is the feeling you get when you know you can stagnate if you remain where you are: that feeling when the top of your head gets hot and your palms sweat, and you know you have to change something.

- **ADVENTUROUS** – I don't believe you should be able to completely visualize the end product. Your project is much like viewing a painting from 50 feet away; you can make out the shape of it, maybe even the subject matter, but the fine details and the style should be part of the journey. I can't say I've ever had any personal project that came out exactly the way I visualized it. Leave space to enjoy the journey on which your work takes you. Allow this work to change you.

• **RECEIVED** – Your goal should be full of intention towards the recipient. There should be a purposeful recipient(s) of your project. Ask yourself, who do I intend to give this gift to? What will others gain from your project? What will I gain at the end? The sole purpose of your project could be to give yourself a shot of courage to complete another project, then another, etc. Or it could be to provide an editorial on the human state, world politics, or religion. Identify your audience. Name your gift.

• **TOUGH** – As Mark Murphy states, "A great goal should make you at least a twinge nervous. It should produce a feeling of 'can I really complete this?'" After all, it's not the easy goals that give us confidence to do more; it's the goals that we surprise even ourselves by completing.

WHAT?

"When we are motivated by goals that have deep meaning, by dreams that need completion, by pure love that needs expressing, then we truly live."

-Greg Anderson

Now comes the fun part. It's time to dream. We talked about the desire and cause of why we create or set goals in the first place. Now it's time to narrow in on the "what," which is: *what* is your goal or project?

Jason Smithers

CHAPTER 3

Finger Farm

Nubie Yom (WAALI)

*"Literally translated as "finger farm." The home,
business, or especially the farm of a person who never
finishes projects but rather points out (hence, finger)
where he or she intends to start new projects and where
things will go in the future."*[1]

NUBIE YOM. I LOVE THE TERM. Mainly because I can
relate to it. I can recall so many conversations in which
people told me about their lofty creative plans, but a year
later none had been touched, let alone completed. I often
think that the failure to complete these good ideas stems
from our desire to impress others at the moment of
explanation, but not in finding fulfillment in the creating that
follows. We take pride in being called "farmers," but we
really don't care to farm. We'd rather just talk about it.

FIND SOMETHING NEW

I'm a musician. I have a degree in music theory and performance. I love music. I love writing and performing music. My primary instrument is the guitar, but over the years I've come to the realization that I don't identify myself as a guitarist. I began playing around the age of 12. Not because I loved the instrument. I had other motives. My dad liked guitar so I wanted to do something that would make him proud. We saw incredible jazz musicians together. He loved it. Truth be told, I didn't. I stuck with guitar because I realized I was actually pretty good at it, and that proficiency earned me some recognition through high school and most of my twenties. It was a massive self-esteem booster. It was also a massive ego boost, which was bad. I only really practiced when I needed to for a performance and rarely out of enjoyment. Why did I stick with something for so long if I didn't love it? Because there was a transaction that occurred. When I would play, I was given the spotlight, or sometimes even pay. I was also given an identity. I was a "guitarist" and there's a certain feeling of pride that swells up in a person when they can identify with something "cool" like being a guitarist.

But now, 20 years after picking up my first guitar, none of my life's personal goals are focused on the guitar, because I realized a few years ago that playing doesn't bring me a complete sense of personal fulfillment. Songwriting does. And you know what instrument I don't really touch when I write songs? That's right. The guitar. I've written and co-written more than 150 songs over the past five years, but the majority of them have been written on piano. I write on the piano because I don't understand the instrument very well. I don't know it inside and out like I do the guitar, so everything feels new and fresh. I approach things differently. If I were to write songs on guitar, they would just be old tricks and hooks that I've been recycling for the past 20 years. They are good songs, but they aren't great. With the piano, I surprise myself. I feel composing songs on piano is a lot like meeting a stranger for the first time. Some days I sit down and the conversation is short, awkward, and goes nowhere. Some days I find out the stranger's background is very interesting. I find a chord or a melody that goes somewhere, and the conversation becomes rich and meaningful. I chose to put down the guitar, something I'm way more proficient at that produces good songs, in exchange for the piano, which I barely know how to play, but it produces better ideas.

THE BUFFET

Maybe you are a lot like me where you've been doing a craft for 20 years that you are too familiar with. It's to the point that you know every technique and approach so well that nothing excites you; nothing surprises you. Maybe you are a good murder-mystery screenplay writer, but your well of creative plots has run dry. Maybe you are a musician like me, and your current instrument of choice has lost its luster. If that's your story, then it's time to hit the buffet.

About two years ago, I had the privilege of a twenty-minute conversation with author and CEO of Breather, Julien Smith. Julien Smith wrote a fantastic book titled <u>The Flinch</u> that truly changed my life. The book deals with why we hesitate to take on the challenges in life that could lead us down rewarding paths. I can't recommend this book enough.

Julien gave me twenty minutes of his time to ask him anything. The first thing I asked was, "I'm ready to not flinch in tackling and completing creative projects, but at 29 years old, I don't even know what to focus on. How do I pick a route and stick with it?"

Julien's advice was this: "For a time, treat life like a buffet. Sample everything, put it all on your plate, experience flavors you may or may not like." As a creative, this could be translated as, "Try new art forms! Try them all!" If you are stuck as a painter, try writing music. If you are a computer programmer or web designer, try creative writing. Many brilliant artists have found their voice by switching art forms. As a creative, you aren't defined by your craft; you are defined by the way your brain functions and processes the world.

Some of us have had the luck in life to be forced out of a craft that we were good at and must then pursue something great. In 1919, a young Walt Disney worked on editorial cartoons for the Kansas City Star and was subsequently fired from the job. His boss stated he "lacked imagination."[2]

Back in 1982, The Beastie Boys released an EP entitled *Polly Wog Stew*. Their earlier work sounds *nothing* like their later extremely influential album, <u>License to Ill</u>. They started off as a heavy punk rock band and found a niche by experimenting, going to the buffet and throwing a bunch of genres on their plate. The result was a sound that was half hip-hop, half punk. They helped change the game for the next 25 years.

You aren't defined as a creator by your craft. The craft you are most proficient at may have just been the first outlet you latched on to. Think about this: what if you have the ability to write deeply rich screenplays and you don't even know it? What if you are, by trade, a musician, but could uncover a deep passion for film — you just haven't had the exposure or circle of influence to know any better?

For all of us, I'm suggesting a 30-day challenge. For 30 days, I want you to hit the buffet. I want you to try a craft that you've never touched. I want you to pick up an instrument you've never played. I want you to reach for a pen instead of a paintbrush.

Below I'm going to provide some resources on how to do this:

The Unfinished Community (Facebook Group)
This is a closed group I've created on Facebook for people to connect with other hopeful creative types trying out this challenge. My hope is that you can connect with other individuals who are stretching themselves in practicing a new medium. The goal is to introduce yourself and share which

new medium you will be trying for the next 30 days. This group provides an opportunity for input and encouragement from others taking this challenge. Share something every day. Post thoughtful insight on how trying a new form of expression is impacting you. For more information on when this group takes place, email info@unfinished.life.

Cousera (https://www.coursera.org)

Coursera is a free online resource in which you can take full courses in the Arts and other professions. I've taken a songwriting course through Coursera. The material was hands-on, and the teaching was practical. By the end of the class, I wrote four songs as homework. You can take classes in Design, Modern & Contemporary Poetry, Architecture, Theater, Video Game Design, and even introductory classes to art and music if you are just starting your creative journey.

Meetup (http://www.meetup.com)

Meetup is a great way to surround yourself with local creatives. You can search your area for local Meetups by interest. Most people on Meetup are non-professionals pursuing a craft on the side. Look at it as a way to be around creatives of a different craft, and decide if you want to become what they are.

30-Day Checklist

If you'd rather tackle this 30-day challenge on your own, then I would challenge you to create a 30-day checklist of various exercises to break you out of your normal routine. Here are a few ideas:

Day One: Draw a nonsense creature, something that a reasonable person couldn't say what it looks like.

Day Two: Write lyrics to a song; don't worry about structure.

Day Three: Try Yoga for 30 minutes.

Day Four: Buy an instrument.

Day Five: Write a one-page story.

Day Six: Take 30 photographs and post to Instagram with the hashtag #30picturesaday.

Day Seven: Try Crossfit.

Day Eight: Quit Crossfit (because it's terrifying).

Day Nine: Buy three albums outside of your normal preferences.

Day Ten: Spend an hour learning to code.

Day Eleven: Write a poem.

Day Twelve: Watch a random documentary.

(A Full 30 Checklist is included in the back of this book)

Journal each day and observe what ignites an interest or passion inside you. Write about what bores you. Which of these days do you never want to repeat? Which of the days would you love to do all the time?

Now, if we all ate at buffets everyday of our lives, we'd have a high likelihood of becoming obese and lethargic from the quantities and varieties we decide to put on our plates. Creative Buffets are only good for a season in life. They are meant to help you narrow down what you truly enjoy, what gives you energy, or what fills your tank after a long day of work or taking care of life's responsibilities. You'll learn so much about yourself going through this adventure.

My biggest realization is that in every craft I've tried, I've always gravitated toward the role of a producer, but I feel as though I've been more of a curator of artists. I enjoy coming alongside brilliant artists and finding projects that we can work on together—projects that show their strengths. I like to watch the big picture come together and cheer them on as the project begins to take on a skin of its own. I wouldn't have known this about myself if I hadn't sought out opportunities to hit the buffet.

YOUR CREATIVE PERSONALITY

In the adventure to find your craft, I encourage you to also onality while creating. You may ask, "Isn't my the work?" Yes, but through this adventure arn so much more about your personality, and knowing your personality type will help you focus on what your unique talents are.

A year ago, I had the pleasure of being mentored under a brilliant Creative Director named Stephen Brewster. He was a thoughtful coach and he helped me through some personal revelations with his introduction of the Eight Types of Creative Personalities. These are geared towards the context of working within a creative team, but I believe these descriptors still translate to individuals working on personal goals.

THE CONCEPTUALIST

A person that processes and passes on their ideas and innovative thoughts to others. Conceptualists are dreamers. They have amazing ideas. Conceptualists often are solution people, problem solvers, and excel in think tanks. They have a unique way of making ideas appear. They create ideas. They can sit down in a meeting and with little or no notice just begin to spout ideas. And not just ideas—really good ideas. They are great at beginning the creative process. The downside to a conceptualist is that as amazing as they are at creating ideas, they are usually not as awesome at actually executing these ideas.

THE ENHANCER

Simply, enhancers make ideas better. They are able to listen to an idea and identify adjustments to make it more effective, creative, sticky, or just better. They help creativity be its absolute best.

THE ARCHITECT

Architects make ideas happen. They are idea builders. Architects are the craft persons of the creative world. They understand the idea and know how to move it from concept to execution. Architects build great teams and identify the necessities of making ideas come to life. They identify talent, connect the right people, and know the timeline for making this happen. They see the end product and know how to work to bring that to life. Architects tend to be inventors or producers by nature.

THE PIONEER

Pioneers are first. They are the early adopters. They are those people who seemingly always know the new song first or identify the latest design trend. They are the people on your team who see that cool YouTube video before everyone else. It is important to identify the pioneer because they refuse to be comfortable. They are always on the lookout, identifying what the next, next, next big thing could or should be. Pioneers collect, share, and broadcast their findings for others and often find identity in knowing what is new. They get bored with what is popular.

THE STORYTELLER

Storytellers create by composing. They identify the story in everything they see. They don't just write, but they understand the art of weaving together the story. Be it a live environment, a video, or the new employment manual, they are composing stories inside of projects. Storytellers articulate the story and wrap ideas in narrative.

38

THE PERFORMER

Performers understand the importance of delivery. They are the people who capture the idea and can keep people motivated and engaged. They inspire people to rally around the idea. When it comes time to share the idea with the rest of the organization, the performer does such a great job sharing the idea that it moves other people to be involved. Performers understand the art of delivery.

THE ANTAGONIST

Antagonists punch holes. While this is not a popular role, it is very necessary. Antagonists ask questions — often uncomfortable questions. They want things to be right and are not usually blinded by the romanticism that surrounds ideas. Antagonists are willing to fight for what's right and are often misunderstood as being stuck in their ways or just plain negative. The trick to working with antagonists is positioning them in a place where they can use their gifts without hurting the morale or energy of the team, giving them permission, and coaching them on the right time to use their gifts. Healthy antagonists have the ability to get onboard with ideas once the ideas are processed and execution begins.

THE CURATOR

The curator sees the big picture. They understand how ideas work together. Curators understand feel and experience. They know which ideas will work, which ideas are not ready, and which ideas might be better used elsewhere. Curators approach art with less emotion but with the filter of how the end user will feel the ideas.

Personally, I resonate the most as a Curator and have been able to say yes or no to personal projects based on whether or not they fit my strength in curating. Don't just choose what personality from this list fits you; we tend to think of ourselves in roles that are not often reality. Ask your friends, family, and co-workers to select which one of these personalities fits you the best. Find one that gets the majority of votes and really dig into how the knowledge of this role can help you select a project.

Once you've spent some time at the buffet, found a path that makes you tick, and determined your primary personality trait, it's time to focus in on a project.

SQUINTING

An Olympic archer trains his whole life to hit the center of a target. At this point in an archer's career, hitting the target isn't a concern; it's where the arrow will land in that target that is the focus. Much like an archer hitting a target, we have laid the groundwork to allow us to create. Now the focus needs to be on what we can create. What will be the focus of our aim? There may be many good projects that we could focus on, but we are now looking for the center of the target – to use the phrase, "Aim small, miss small."

As an archer pulls his string to the center of his chest, he is looking down range, focusing on the center of the target; and not just the center... the center of the center of the center of the target. As the archer does this, he begins to close his non-dominant eye. His field of vision narrows. Then, his dominant eye closes slightly. He squints. Squinting changes the shape of our eyes and lets in only a small amount of light[3]. The field of vision narrows even more, seeking what is important. The center of the center of the target comes completely into focus. Once the target is in focus, the archer releases an arrow intended for that small speck.

Over the years I've come in contact with so many frustrated people who had set out to tackle a project only to fail because their "what" wasn't defined. Their ideas were general and broad. They couldn't put detail to their dreams.

Artist: "I'm going to record an album."

Me: "That's awesome! What's the main feel of the album? What's the subject?"

Artist: "I'm not there yet. It's going to be organic, just writing in the moment and let the end result be whatever."

Me: "Ok, well, good luck with that."

I can almost know without fail which individuals will see a project to completion and which ones will get left on the side of the road by the "muse" with no way to get to the end. In order to get to completion, each part of your project needs to be thought out. Obstacles begin to surface as every facet of the project is examined. It's a way to predict what will stop you from finishing your project and work on solutions to these obstacles.

41

Artist: *"I want to complete an album that makes the listener feel they are in the heart of South Africa, to paint the political landscapes with the lyrics."*

Now the artist has focused in on the center of the center of the target. He or she is now more likely to hit the target because they know what they are aiming at. Listen to Paul Simon talk about his intentions for the now-classic album, <u>Graceland</u>. He was very intentional about putting the listener in the time of Apartheid.

THE QUESTIONS

This is the part I get excited about. The artist and nerd in me latch arms in harmony. This section will be turning your dreams of completing a personal project into the wireframe of what the end project will look like. The nuances that will be your personal touch will come at a later time.

This part should take some time; time soul-searching and asking yourself honest questions about each project idea.

I do yearly goals. Some people only set goals 3-4 months out because the time frame is easier to control, but a year just seems to work for me. During a given year, when an idea for a creative goal comes to me, I'll write it down in an Evernote notebook I have labeled *Possible Goals for Next Year*. At the end of the year, I get out of town for a day and sit down with the previous year's goals and evaluate:

1. Which ones were completed and which goals weren't?

2. Was I passionate and fulfilled by this goal?
    (Answer this for each goal, whether completed or not)

3. If I failed to hit a goal, why do I suppose that was?

This gives me some thoughts as I approach the next year's goals. If I set a goal the year before to write 30 songs and only wrote six, then I really need to wrestle to the ground if it's worth trying again the next year. "Why did I fizzle out so early? Was it the topic? Was I too isolated as a writer? Was I just not that passionate about this one? Do I need to make this year's goal to 'co-write' 30 songs so there's more fuel and accountability to get me through this goal?"

Once I evaluate last year's goals, I'll bring up my Possible Goals folder for the coming year and begin the interrogation process:

"What's the real reason I want to complete this project?"

"Does this fill my ego or help add meaning to my life or others?"

This sounds like arduous work, but this really should be a fun day for you. Carve this day out for yourself where you can turn off your phone, quit out of your email and social media accounts, and just dream! Here's what my day usually looks like:

7am-11am:
Find a new out of town coffee shop and evaluate last year's goals.

11am-Noon:
Roam around town kicking over any new projects I hadn't written down yet in my Evernote folder.

Noon-4pm:
Sit down with my *Possible Goals* folder and hammer out the details of what the finished project would look like.

4pm- 9pm:
Think through the obstacles and timeframe required to complete each goal. Determine if I'd really have the energy/passion to complete it.

Two years ago, I had the idea to write a children's book for my older daughter, Maci, but I'm not anywhere near being a strong illustrator. I knew I was passionate about this goal because I wanted to give my daughter a gift that not every child has: a book for her and about her. Yet, I knew very little about creating a book.

Here's how the goal started that day:

"Goal: Complete a children's book for Maci."

After working through everything, I knew it had to be more defined. Here's what I landed on:

"Co-create and self-publish a fully illustrated, hardcover children's book (minimum 20 pages) for Maci, about Maci, by December 31st of this year."

Sitting down with that goal and asking all the right questions really helped give the goal a workable wireframe.

"Who will illustrate the book?"

"How will I get the book published?"

"Who could help me with storyline and dreaming?"

"Can I complete an entire book in a year without pulling my hair out?"

If I had only written down "complete a book by the end of 2013," I would have been going in blind without a wireframe map. I needed more than a loose concept.

I didn't yet know the complete story arc or style, but I had a good definition of what the successful end product would look like. I had the "what," now I needed to figure out how I was going to complete the book.

In 2013, I completed a 20+ page fully illustrated, hardcover children's book for my daughter Maci, about Maci as the fictional character 'Alora' entitled, *Alora in the Clouds*.

CHAPTER 4

Time To Start

Tsundoku *(JAPANESE)*

"The constant act of buying books and never reading them."[1]

WHO HASN'T BEEN THAT PERSON? We see a title of a book that jumps out to us, and we pick it up thinking it holds what we are looking for in that moment. We are hoping it will tell us what to do next. Just give us some easy steps. If we don't find "the secret to selling a million books" in the first couple pages, we put it aside. We don't necessarily want our projects to be easy; we just want step-by-step instructions on how complete it.

HOW DO YOU START?

I grew up on Legos. I think I can speak for all the 1980s kids out there that Lego is in its Renaissance period right now. The company really found its stride with the 2014 movie, appealing to our nostalgia and connecting with a new audience of young creators. You can now go on Lego's website and find a build for any experience level and interest; anything from Lego *The Lord of the Rings* 2359 piece Tower of Orthanc to the newer architecture line of Legos where you can build famous monuments and buildings. One of the most complicated sets available on their website is the 3803 piece Star Wars Death Star. You can have it for a measly $399.99!

Many say the continued success of Lego over the years is due to how it inspires creativity and the desire for young and young-at-heart builders to build more. But I would argue that their continued success is largely due to their incredibly well laid-out instruction manuals. Lego sells very few sets that are "build whatever you feel like" sandbox kits. Their money is in retro-creating projects into well-known forms, like the Death Star, and instructing you how to do it yourself. We can all agree that Lego wouldn't be around long if their Death Star kit only included a single picture of a completed Death Star and a pile of pieces. Very few of us would complete it or even know where to begin!

We love Legos because they hold our hand through the building process, and along the way we are shown clever ways to build our own structures. Many branch off from the Lego kit's final form after completing it once and build their own interpretations (I personally like my roomy and relaxing Death Star Hotel).

It would be great if every creative project we took on had a manual of the steps along the way like a Lego set, but our personal projects are our own. We are the architects. We have to build the plans, and it's not a blueprint that should be done along the way. I believe success in completing personal projects lies in creating blueprints and roadmaps before we begin.

When I decided I wanted to do this book, I just started writing. It was bad; even my friends told me so. I didn't have a direction, and they could tell. Noting that I knew far less about writing a non-fiction book than I thought I did, I scrapped the earlier writings and started over. This time, I followed this process before writing another word:

STEP 1: Knowledge (Understanding, Education, Skills)

I spent a couple of months reading a few books on writing non-fiction (I would highly recommend *Bird by Bird* by Anne Lamott[2] and *The Clockwork Muse* by Eviatar Zerubavel[3] if your goal is also based in writing long form). I took notes on approach and, in doing so, demystified the writing process. I now felt confident in how to restart.

STEP 2: Blueprint (Organize, Plan, Layout, Map)

The next step for me was to gather all my topics and organize them into sections and sub sections (this has changed somewhat as I wrote this, but for the most part, stayed a "true north" direction for me). Once I knew *what* I was going to write about, I created a deadline for everything.

STEP 3: Deadline (Timeframe, Zero Hour)

Each section of the book was broken down into when I was going to complete them. Setting deadlines for yourself in personal work is such a critical step, and it is paramount to do whatever you can to keep those deadlines. We will get into specifics of why this is such a critical part of every personal project in a later section.

TINY DRUGS

Back in the early 1980s, Curtis Tyler, Alex Smith, and Conrad Will decided that the distances that make up the most mind boggling endurance challenge, The Ironman just weren't long enough: 2.4-mile (3.86 km) swim, a 112-mile (180.25 km) bicycle ride and a marathon 26.2-mile (42.2 km) run. From this incomprehensible notion, the first Ultraman Race was born in 1983.

This event is limited to 40 athletes by invite only. The athletes converge on the big island of Hawaii for this three-day race. Day one consists of a 6.2-mile ocean swim followed by a 90-mile cross-country bike ride. Day two gets just a 'little' tougher with a 171.4-mile (276-km) bike ride with a vertical climb of 4,000 feet. Day three, the final leg of the race, consists of a Double. Marathon. You read that right — 52.4-mile run[4]. This is, as its name suggests, the absolute pinnacle of testing the endurance of a human's limits.

When you watch an Olympic race, what's the first thing the winner does? The top finisher throws his or her hands in the air in victory. Observing athletes cross the finish line of the Ultraman race, many throw their hands up in victory because the race isn't about first.

It's about finishing.

Throwing the hands in the air is the product of a chemical reaction happening at that moment in each competitor's brain. Minds are pushed past the mental limits to maintain focus and keep the legs moving, and crossing the finish line is the equivalent of releasing the air from a balloon. Tension leaves the body, and arms stretch to the air. Milliseconds before the hands raise, exhausted bodies are treated with a massive surge of the chemical dopamine. Dopamine is a neurotransmitter responsible for the warm, fuzzy feeling of achievement we get when we are presented with gifts, rewards, or upon completion of a difficult task[5]. The more monumental the task is perceived, the more we feel the effects of dopamine. Illegal narcotics also release the same chemical. If the effects of dopamine can hook someone on an illegal substance, it may also have the power to hook us on completing our goals.

To do this, it makes sense to turn our large goal into a collection of sub-goals thus providing us with positive reinforcement along the way towards finishing our work. The more progress we make towards completing the large goal, the larger our motivation grows.

When I started tracking my goals back in 2009, I started with five main goals. In 2014, I realized I set 23 main goals for myself, which meant at least 276 sub goals had been set. If completing goals releases dopamine like an illegal narcotic, that only meant one thing: I was legitimately addicted to goal setting.

Think of setting smaller goals as setting live (humane) traps for your brain. To catch a wild animal with a live trap, you have to lead it to a cache of food with smaller morsels along the way. The animal will first pick up the scent of the smaller morsels, then begin nibbling at the first piece in the trail, followed by the second piece and so on until it's led into the cage by the sight of a feast. Once the animal steps on a trigger plate, the cage closes, and it's caught without injury. When we set smaller goals for ourselves that lead to the big payoff, we are giving our brains bait to keep it pushing our work forward.

THE CHECKLIST TRAP

When you watch an animal pick up the scent and approach the first morsel, it's tentative. It looks around to make sure it's not going to be attacked by a larger animal in search of the same food. It will sniff around for any alien scents. If the coast is clear, it will try the first bite.

When planning out your smaller goals, you'll want to set them up like a live trap – a Checklist Trap. Your first task should be something easy, something that won't cause you to run in the opposite direction of your work. Make this task something that can be completed in under an hour with very little brainpower or creative thought. You might feel a little silly at first writing examples like the following:

"String up and tune guitars."

"Clear desk of clutter, set out laptop."

"Buy 10 11x14 Canvases."

From here, make the next step toward completing your goal a bit tougher — something that will take some creative brainpower and a little more time:

"Compile a list of songs for creative inspiration."

"Set aside two hours to write a rough synopsis."

"Begin a mood board of styles and textures for inspiration."

Through the process, we are leading our brains toward the big goal. We are earning trust and confidence in the process. We are completing very easy tasks to build momentum.

I've previously mentioned *The Clockwork Muse* by Eviatar Zerubavel[6] and I used tips from Eviatar's book to write *this* book. To complete my first draft, I broke it down to the following steps:

1. Read two books about writing a work of non-fiction.

2. Take 2 hours to do a short synopsis on the subject.

3. Create an outline.

4. Break the book down into chapters.

5. Break the chapters down into sections.

Once I completed these tasks, I then set a schedule to finish each section. I would sit down and try to write 2 sections, typically in a 2-3 hour block twice a week, using this template from *The Clockwork Muse*:

Section	Length (words)	Words Per Day	Days to complete	Deadline
Introduction	1,000	500	2	3/02/15
Chapter 1	2,000	500	4	3/20/15
Chapter 2	2,500	1,000	2.5	4/07/15
Chapter 3	2,500	1,000	2.5	4/21/15
Chapter 4	2,500	500	5	5/15/15
Chapter 5	4,000	1000	4	5/30/15

A Checklist Trap can work with any creative project as long as it can be broken down to small tasks you can check off along the way. If you are skeptical, here's an example of a short project broken down into very easy-to-complete tasks:

PAINTING A LANDSCAPE

1. Pin 20 pictures on Pinterest for inspiration.

2. Buy an 11x11 canvas.

3. Make sure I have enough paint.

4. Take 15 minutes to set up my workstation.

5. Sketch a rough idea for 20 minutes.

6. Work for 30 minutes on the left quadrant of the painting.

...and so on.

Checklist Traps are the reason we LOVE the late artist, Bob Ross. Ross was one of the first artists to reveal his Checklist Traps on national television. Before the show, if I saw a completed Bob Ross painting, I would laugh at you if you told me I could make a fairly decent rendition of his work in 30 minutes.

He broke the process down into the smallest tasks — the simplest brush strokes, the "happiest little tree." If you could put paint on your brush and move it from side to side, you could have a serene forest scene fit for Bambi in as much time as it took to watch Family Ties.

Deconstructing large bodies of work down to their smallest tasks puts us that much closer to being as prolific and masterful as the great Bob Ross.

CHAPTER 5

Effort(less)?

Sprezzatura *(ITALIAN)*

"Sprezzatura is an Italian word originating from Baldassare Castiglione's The Book of the Courtier, where it is defined by the author as 'a certain nonchalance, so as to conceal all art and make whatever one does or says appear to be without effort and almost without any thought about it'."[1]

START WITH UNINVITING

WE TAKE FAMILY DINNERS AROUND THE TABLE
SERIOUSLY. That old faux mahogany 4-seater table is our
family's Situation Room. It's a time where we can bring up
anything that's been on our minds. Our children are still
young, so we break the ice with "Family Question Time." For
the most part, this stays pretty silly with questions like:
"Would you rather be a hotdog or a spaghetti noodle?" "If
you could only eat one type of candy for the rest of your life,
what would it be?" (The correct answer is Sour Patch Kids, if
you were wondering). But silly sometimes leads to serious.
The silly questions will trigger a thought or emotion out of
one of our kids that they will want to talk about and unpack.
This now feels organic and natural, but we had to make the
table a sacred space. We don't allow phones at the table; we
don't allow TV or music during dinner — nothing that would
distract an important topic from coming to the surface. What
you invite to the table will have your attention.

Time with our creative work is much like a dinner
conversation with a loved one. Our work once had our
attention at the table. The conversations were entertaining,
but often lead to deep, meaningful time in our memories.
They may have been the child who was often boisterous or
delightfully entertaining to watch. They may have been the
friend we could have hours of conversation with and lose
track of time, but we've filled their seat at the table with
everything from apathy, fear, and busyness to scrolling social
networks for hours on end. Our passions are standing with
arms folded, tapping their foot waiting to be at the table

again; waiting for our undivided attention, but we complain that there just isn't a place for them to sit anymore.

Before our personal projects can have a seat at the table again, something else has to get up. If we are going to complete our work, then we need that valuable space and time our distractions are taking up.

Some things occupying that seat may even seem like good things: the extra job, community events, coffee with friends, errands we have to run; but I don't think there's a single person that would argue with me when I say that when we try to do too much, then nothing gets our complete focus. I'm not saying these things have to be completely out of your life; they just can't be at the table when you are working. For a time, some relationships and activities may need to take a sabbatical.

Greg McKeown wrote one of the most important books of the last 10 years on this subject entitled, "*Essentialism: The Disciplined Pursuit of Less*," in which McKeown states, "Multitasking itself is not the enemy . . . pretending we can 'multi-focus' is."[2]

Back in 2014, I tried to do everything. I was Creative Director at a church in Melbourne, Florida while also Creative Producer for a company in Orlando. On the side, I was pursuing freelance work as a photographer and music producer. I'd also just released my first book, and an EP with The Science Class. On top of all this, we had moved into a new community, a new home, and had a new baby!

To say I was stretched to the point of exhaustion would be an understatement. Don't get me wrong; I'm certainly blessed that all of these things were good and fit within the "creative" realm, but they weren't all great. They weren't all producing fruit, and my focus was all over the map.

During a family vacation, I was taking long conference calls with the company in Orlando and realized this pace was insane. My passions and family weren't getting my attention. I had to cut things out to sharpen my focus on just a few great things, but I really didn't know how to decide what to cut and what to keep. My wife came to the rescue by creating a formula that changed my life. The following exercise will help you sharpen your focus on what is truly worth your time.

STEP ONE:
Write out every large item that has your attention at the moment in a column sheet (see the example). This would include hobbies, side jobs, places you volunteer, etc.

Step 1. Example

Writing			
Music Production			
Full-Time Job			
Coding			
Side-Job			

STEP TWO:

In the top row, write out the top three to five things that are most important to you in life. Here are some examples of possible categories: Low Stress, Good Pay, Time, Flexibility, Stress, Passion, and Potential for Growth.

Step 2. Example

	Low Stress	Good Pay	Flexibility
Writing			
Music Production			
Full-Time Job			
Coding			
Side-Job			

STEP THREE:

We are going to assign a multiplier number to each of these values in life, ranging from one to three. If low-stress level is important to you, then you would give "Low Stress" a three. If "Good Pay" isn't a large priority in your life, then you would give it a multiplier of one.

Step 3. Example

	Low Stress (x3)	Good Pay (x1)	Flexibility (x2)
Writing			
Music Production			
Full-Time Job			
Coding			
Side-Job			

STEP FOUR:

On a scale of one to ten, write out how well each of your activities from your left column fare in these categories. For example, if you chose "Low Stress" as being important to you, and writing is more of a joy than stress, you would grade writing very high in that column. However, if writing doesn't really bring in a lot of money, you would grade writing low in "Good Pay."

Step 4. Example

	Low Stress (x3)	Good Pay (x1)	Flexibility (x2)
Writing	10	3	5
Music Production	7	2	8
Full-Time Job	3	8	9
Coding	4	7	6
Side-Job	3	7	5

STEP FIVE:

Multiply the numbers from your activity rows (Writing, Producing Music, etc.) with the multiplier from your top columns (Low Stress, Good Pay, etc.) and add up the totals for each activity.

Step 5. Example

	Low Stress (x3)	Good Pay (x1)	Flexibility (x2)	TOTALS
Writing	10x3=30	3x1=3	5x5=10	43
Music Prod.	7x3=21	2x1=2	8x2=16	39
FT Job	3x3=9	8x1=8	9x2=18	35
Coding	4x3=12	7x1=7	6x2=12	31
Side-Job	3x3=9	7x1=7	5x2=10	26

STEP SIX: (The Fun Part)

Take the two lowest scoring activities and throw them out of your life. I mean it. You can't argue with the numbers. If you have too many things in your life, then it makes sense that the least fruitful things need to be cut to make more time and space for the most fruitful.

Step 6. Example

Writing	43
Music Prod.	39
Full-time Job	35
~~Coding~~	~~31~~
~~Side Job~~	~~26~~

After completing this exercise, I knew there were two to three activities I needed to cut out of my life. When I arrived home from vacation, I turned in my two weeks notice with the creative agency and shut down two of my freelance websites.

RHYTHM OF WORK

Dinner time has the great distinction of always falling in the same window for most people from 5pm-10pm. Any earlier, and the label changes to "late-lunch" or "I just really want a burger because I'm stressed" time. Our bodies keep us set on a pretty great natural rhythm of when we should eat, but our body does a poor job of alerting us when to create. And unlike dinner, that time to create is very different for many people. There are plenty of resources out there that can help you to find when your natural time of day is to create.

Mine is midday. Some people's most productive time may be morning, others at 2 am, but the rhythm and flow of when you work is just as important as how you work. When playing with a band, if one of the musicians slips a little behind a beat, it's not overtly noticeable as long as they get back on it. A seasoned musician can find his way back to the "1" beat or the start of the progression; but if the musician can't find it, or if they aren't seasoned, they may lose the progression and/or the phrase — and the song may become a train wreck.

This is the same as the rhythm in which you work on your project. If you've set a schedule, you may be ok to start late once or twice, maybe a half hour here or there. It's pretty easy to get back on the horse, but the more days you fall out of rhythm, the harder it will be to get back on track. And sadly, those that try to start over on the one beat have lost the momentum to keep plugging away.

They've lost the song.

When we sit down to work, we aren't promised that time will be fruitful. The truth of the matter is that sitting down to do your work may sometimes be the worst part of your day. In writing this book, I've had multiple writing sessions that I hated, which caused me to lose self-confidence. Self-doubt crept in. But I still showed up.

We've all heard quotes like this from Regina Brett:

"Most of life is showing up. You do the best you can, which varies from day to day."

But few of us think this pertains to our personal projects. Usually we think that we are showing up so our boss can account for our consistency and dedication. Rarely do we think it pertains to "showing up" to our desk, by ourselves, with no one to mark our attendance on a piece of paper, and putting in whatever work we can for those two to three-hour sessions. I challenge you to set a schedule for yourself and show up consistently for a month. Keep a small journal about your sessions, especially during the first few sessions. Write down how you feel. Are you happy with that day's session? What did you learn? What's frustrating you about your project? Keep a record for a month of showing up, even if it just reads, "Sat down a half-hour and couldn't focus, had no original ideas, checked Facebook instead." Watch what happens as time goes by. Working on your project starts more quickly and will feel more natural. Locking into a rhythm will come the more consistently you show up.

WORK IN SECRET

You clear your beautiful, fake mahogany desk, set your favorite Moleskine journal down, and align your pen with the flow of the faux wood grain. Next, you set down the fair-trade coffee so that it balances out the tiny desk plant you've added to the frame, keeping close attention to the "Rule of Thirds."

You're all set.

To work?

Oh, no. Not yet.

Not until the world knows that you are indeed embarking on a journey. This moment will symbolize the beginning of a journey that will materialize into your first album that will be loved by the masses. You won't touch that pen until you've put a nice, grey-scale filter on that picture for social media that emotes the "I'm deep and in tune with the writing process" look you are going for. You post the picture. Hashtag #songwriting #thegrind #dreamsarework #lovemeplease #myofficefortheday

You sit back and smile an inward smile to yourself after hitting send. You've told the world you are working towards a big goal. You feel a sense of achievement even before writing one word for your album that will be a blend of Beck meets Fleetwood Mac meets Abba (that part is a little fuzzy still). You repeat this process a handful of times, but each time you sit down to work, the process seems to get harder. It's stressful and you keep hitting a wall a mere twenty minutes into each session. After the fourth or fifth session and a measly 34 likes on your last Instagram picture, you put the project to the side (you knew you should have taken a selfie next to the mic instead). Blame the lack of inspiration or use excuses like, "my idea is just so complex in my head that it's tough to get it out."

You shelve the Moleskine and walk away from the album you were once so excited about.

So what happened?

Here's what happened. You cheated yourself.

By sharing with the world signs of starting an album before the process began, you withdrew a small amount of currency from the "sense of completion fund" that was only to be accessed once you finished the project. You are getting that small dopamine pay-off without doing any actual creative work. The more times you withdraw from that account, the less exciting it is to complete your goal.

Derek Sivers, the creator of CD Baby backs up this concept with his brilliant, but short TED Talk entitled: *Keep your goals to yourself.*

He brings to the forefront studies done by Peter Gollwitzer. Below is a portion of his transcript from the TED Talk:

> *"It goes like this: 163 people across four separate tests — everyone wrote down their personal goal. Then half of them announced their commitment to this goal to the room, and half didn't. Then everyone was given 45 minutes of work that would directly lead them towards their goal, but they were told that they could stop at any time. Now, those who kept their mouths shut worked the entire 45 minutes, on average, and when asked afterwards, said that they felt that they had a long way to go still to achieve their goal. But those who had announced it quit after only 33 minutes, on average, and when asked afterwards, said that they felt much closer to achieving their goal."[3]*

> *"Announcing your plans to others satisfies your self-identity just enough that you're less motivated to do the hard work needed."*
>
> *-Derek Sivers*

While writing this chapter, only four people know I'm working towards finishing this book. The only reason they know I am writing this is that they are also playing a part in helping me write this book as editors. My mom doesn't even know I'm in the process of writing (sorry, Mom). When I finished my first children's book, *Alora In the Clouds*, only about 10 people knew what I was doing, and just like this book, all of those people were in on the process. I knew if I shared what I was doing early on with friends and family, I would only be satisfying my ego and need to validate my self-worth, thus lessening the likelihood of completion.

THE PRESSURE AND THE LETDOWN

I didn't always do this. I loved to be the guy to jump on social media and tell the world what I was doing. But once I threw my goals out to the world, I felt this unnecessary pressure in my creative process, as though the whole conglomerate of the Internet was now awaiting my project. I thought it would work to my advantage as some sort of accountability, but instead it walled off my thoughts and added phantom critics in my head. "Now that this person knows I'm working on something, they are probably ready to tear it to shreds once it's finished." I would turn my work into something that would appease the phantom critics, but always come up short of the perceived quality bar I built in my head.

Along with phantom critics, I also created phantom fans — people in my head that were just waiting by the "pre-order" button on Amazon for my next project to come out. As I fell further and further behind on any progress, I felt like I was letting them down. In reality, the only person that was probably waiting by the Amazon 1-click was my mom (Hi, again, Mom).

The reality is, unless you are someone world-famous with a track record of amazing work, chances are people aren't waiting to tear you to shreds, nor are they waiting in line to buy your next work. So why not wait to tell everyone until it's at least 90% complete?

Still need another reason to keep your goals to yourself? How about this: it's actually a lot of fun! By not sharing your goals, you take on a bit of a secret agent persona. You leave parties early to get home and get to the hard work. Some people will begin to gossip, maybe even think you are doing something morally reprehensible on the side; but really, who cares what they think as long as you are getting closer and closer to finishing your "Beckwood Mac" rock opera? Eight months later you emerge from your cavern to tell the world, "I've finished something I want to share with you."

Unfortunately, a sad thing happens when successful people have completed their goals in secret. People begin to reason that this kind of stuff is just EASY for you. "He whipped up this amazing rock opera with 17 part harmonies and early vibes of Dancing Queen meets Loser. I guess some people are just born gifted."

Enter the "Sprezzatura." That perceived nonchalance was really hustle and grind in secret. You've toiled away for eight months through self-doubt and frustration to emerge with something that makes you proud of your hard work, and people think you were just "born with it."

That's why we are so taken aback when we find out our favorite celebrities have hidden "talents." We think since we've never heard celebrities talk about these abilities, that they just happened to try something new one day and realized they were naturals.

Justin Bieber can solve a Rubik's Cube in less than two minutes. Steve Martin is a phenomenal banjo player and has even won a Grammy for his 2010 album, "The Crow: New Songs for the 5-String Banjo." People, this proficiency didn't happen overnight.

Let them think what they want. Let the "Sprezzatura" linger. You know the truth and can now withdraw the full glory from the "Sense of Completion" fund.

Jason Smithers

CHAPTER 6

The Middle

Seigneur-Terraces *(FRENCH)*

"Coffee shop dwellers who sit at tables a long time but spend little money."[1]

IT'S FITTING THAT I SHOULD DISCUSS THE HALFWAY POINT of your work exactly halfway through this book, because I can relate to how you are feeling. In any project, it's the make-or-break point. Some will power through the middle of the project, but for most people, the dead center of any project is exactly that: the **dead** center. It's where most projects go to die. I'm feeling it right now. I'm the guy sitting in the local coffee shop, and four hours and a $1.90 cup of coffee later; I'm stuck. Staring at my screen, hating everything I'm writing, not sure where to go next, and honestly not even sure if I want to complete this book.

"Standing in the middle of the road is very dangerous; you get knocked down by the traffic from both sides."

-*Margaret Thatcher*

In J.R.R Tolkein's classic novel, *The Hobbit*, around the midpoint of the book, the adventure of Bilbo and his band of dwarves takes them to the edge of the Mirkwood forest. Here, they part ways with their traveling companion, Gandalf, but not before he gives them the key on how to make it through Mirkwood: "Straight through the forest is your way now. Don't stray off the track! If you do, it is a thousand to one you will never find it again and never get out of Mirkwood."[2]

Bilbo and the dwarves spend days on end sticking to the path until they begin to run out of food and start to see visions of elves at a feast. Instead of sticking to the path, they follow their hunger towards the visions. Instead of a feast, they find themselves wrapped up in giant spider webs. If they listened to Gandalf's instructions, and trusted someone who had more experience than they had in the forest, their story may have gone differently.

This is the best analogy that comes to mind in how we treat the middle of our own adventures through our personal projects. So far, we've been given the tools to follow the roadmap of our work toward completion. We've been warned of traps along the way that want to pull us off course. "Just follow the path," we've been told. But the motivation we had at the beginning of the project is running out. Our endorphins are further depleting. We don't like anything about the project anymore and we aren't even sure we want to complete it. We are *hungry* for re-affirmation, confidence and inspiration—so hungry that we start veering off course. We start looking for other ways to get fed. This is the spider's trap. This is the enemy.

> *"In the middle of the journey of our life I came to myself within a dark wood where the straight way was lost."*
>
> -Dante Alighieri

THE ENEMY

Everyone's enemy uses a different type of trick. Mine comes in the form of self-doubt, and it usually creeps into my thoughts through seemingly good avenues. While writing this book, I immersed myself in great authors. I looked for pointers and the things that made their work stand out. I've learned ways to write naturally and humorously without it feeling forced through authors like Jon Acuff and Anne Lamott. Reading Malcolm Gladwell taught me how having case studies within your work keep it interesting. I've recognized how Donald Miller can seem to pull the "that's how I feel!" relatability from his readers in his storytelling. For me, these authors act as roadmaps to completing a good work. But as I read them, voices off the beaten path are telling me, "Wow, this is masterful writing. What business do you have trying to put a book together? You know approximately 211 words in the English language. You write like a caveman compared to Orson Scott Card or Viktor Frankl. Maybe you should just consider quitting now. You got halfway through. That's pretty good. You have enough content for like 5 or 6 blog posts. Why not just go that route? No one reads long form anymore anyway."

Quitting now would be easy. As I stated before, only a handful of people knew I was doing this in the first place so what would it affect anyway? You may relate to this feeling. Or you may relate more to "bigger and better" things falling into your path. After all, the frustrating middle of your project is way less sexy than a new opportunity in front of you. So you repeat this pattern. You chase beginnings until the next exciting thing comes along.

Whatever your enemy to staying on the path is, we all have them. We just do a horrible job labeling them. It's important that we can label our enemies so we can develop strategies to defend against them.

Go through all your failed projects in the past and be honest with yourself with these questions:

1. At what point in the process did I get frustrated or distracted?

2. What excuses did I make to not power through the middle?

3. What or whom is my worst enemy?

TRICKS TO CLIMBING OUT OF THE VALLEY

It's only fitting that it's been two weeks between writing the last section about the enemy and writing this section. I'm dead center in the middle of this book and didn't heed my own advice. "I'll just take today off. I've got time tomorrow to write. I need a break." I tricked myself while in the MIDST of writing about the enemy.

That's the equivalent of telling a new parent that they should never, I mean, never go to Chuck E. Cheese on a Saturday at noon, while sitting in the vomit-filled ball pit at noon on a Saturday. It doesn't matter how much you work out, if you take a week or two off, it takes a lot of willpower and trickery to get your butt back to the gym.

There are a thousand different articles about how to find the energy to get back in the gym. My favorite is the one in which they tell you to get changed into your gym clothes. Just that action gets you closer to the gym. I mean, you are in your clothes now, might as well hit the gym, right? I don't know how many episodes of "The West Wing" I binged while sitting in my gym clothes eating Taco Bell.

Tricks like that can be effective. Just get out your brushes and paint supplies and hopefully from there your willpower will do the rest. Sometimes this works. Sometimes it doesn't. I've developed a few more "tricks" to get back on track when the enemy gets the best of me.

CREATE A MASTERMIND JURY

In Napoleon Hill's now-classic book *Think and Grow Rich*, he introduced us to the principle of the Mastermind. The principle suggests that we can achieve our goals with far better success when we are "in harmony" or rather, in community with a group who shares the same interests, goals, dreams. When I started to look at my favorite artists, I realized they all had this beautiful community in place.

Between the 1930s and 1940s a group that called themselves The Inklings met in a small pub in Oxford called The Eagle and Child. The Inklings would meet on Tuesdays and discuss literary fiction[3]. So who were some of The Inklings? C.S. Lewis and J.R.R. Tolkien, among others. It's been said that C.S. Lewis distributed early versions of *The Lion, The Witch and The Wardrobe* to the group and Tolkien read portions of *The Hobbit* and *The Lord of the Rings* to the group.

Can you imagine being there in that moment when Tolkien is introducing his friends to Bilbo Baggins, a *Hobbit*, for the very first time? I would have paid a lot of money to hear the reactions and opinions. "Hey, Ronald, I like where you are going with this whole adventure thing, but what about instead of these Hobbit creatures, you made them more, ya know, normal? Like '*There and Back Again, A Normal Guy's Story?*' I don't know, the big, hairy feet just weird me out a little. I mean, I'm just C.S. Lewis, author of *The Chronicles of Narnia*, what do *I* know? Just something to think about."

If you've been privileged enough to spend any bit of time in a group that challenges, inspires, and motivates you to create more often and better, then you should consider yourself blessed for as long as you were/are able to be in that community. If you haven't found it yet, stop everything now and *find one*. I'll help you. Email me at jason@unfinished.life, and you and I will find one together.

These Mastermind groups can be massively effective at helping you get to the end of your goal, but I have one problem with this system. There's no consequence for not finishing. In the end, the only power the group has is to encourage you to keep trying. So I've made an adjustment to the Mastermind groups I run. I call them Mastermind Juries.

WANT TO FINISH? PAY SOMEONE

"If you are having a hard time getting over a fence, throw your boot over it. Cause now, giving up isn't an option."

-My Friend's Grandma

Mastermind groups are fantastic for the majority of people, but if you require more accountability, then you need to give your accountability groups the power to go to the next level. You need to give them the power to punish for not completing your work. When we miss a credit car we are punished. When we are caught disobeying we are punished. These punishments start wit escalate from there. For the majority of us, the possibility of losing our hard-earned money is reason enough to keep current with our bills and maintain the speed limit. So why not set up a few laws surrounding your project? (I know, sounds fun, right?)

Try this: find someone you know that can keep you accountable and is in your corner for you to complete your project. Write them a check, send them money via Paypal, or give them cash to hold on to. If you don't finish an agreed-upon mile marker by a certain date, then they get to keep the money. Suggestions for mile markers could be:

x number of pages written
x number of songs written
x photos shot and edited
x number of steps taken to finish a painting

You get the idea. Also, make sure the amount of money they are holding onto hurts a bit. Meaning, it's going to keep you up at night and keep you working to hit your goal because you absolutely cannot lose that money.

Make a pact with the person holding the money that they won't be swayed to return the money no matter how many excuses you give them as to why you couldn't hit your goal.

As I'm writing this, I'm actually under one of these agreements. I will lose 150 dollars to my good friend Micah if I don't complete 3,000 words of this book by tomorrow at *midnight.

*(Midnight' was word number 2,994. I. Just. Need. Three. More. COMPLETE!)

QUIT DIGGING DOWN

When many of us are in the valley of our work, we are told to keep pushing forward and digging in, but that's terrible advice if the direction you are digging in is down.

Kids are stubborn and a great example of digging down. My youngest daughter Addie has a playhouse with a door and a window. She also has a stuffed puppy she likes to take into the playhouse. The problem is that nine times out of ten, she tries to push the puppy through the window when the door is right next to her. She pushes, and the puppy gets stuck. So what does she do? She tries to push it even more! It's not helpful for me as a parent to shout out motivational sayings while she's trying to push the puppy through the window like, "You can do it, Addie!" "Reach for your dreams!" "The window is just an obstacle!" No, my goal is to show her a better way, a different approach to her end goal. "Hey Addie, see the big opening next to the one that you are popping a vein in your forehead to push your puppy through? Yea, try that one instead."

TAKE STEPS BACKWARD

Sometimes we get so stuck in a project that we don't look around us and realize the way out of the valley is right next to us. If you are stuck, stop pushing and ask for other perspectives. Use your mastermind jury. Your peers may have a different perspective—a vantage point to see from that you can't see. Often, when I get stuck on a project, I ask my peers what they think. Your friends will be more than happy to lend their thoughts, but you have to be willing to listen with open ears even if it means taking a few steps back.

In music production, I'm a bit of a rusher. I like to get in, work, and not tinker with things too much; but sometimes I just hit this wall where I can't think of what to do next, so I'll bypass a problem only to create more problems. By the time I've finished 75% of a song I realize nothing is cohesive. The verse doesn't build into a chorus that builds into a great bridge. I'm stuck, and going forward seems pointless because the rest of the song seems to go nowhere.

My co-producer friend, Jeff Harris, is the opposite, and I hate it. I groan when he finds a problem with the song because I know it won't mean fixing that part; it means that we'll have to fix the part before that and the part before that. I find myself arguing with him and convincing myself that those other parts are fine. What I'm really arguing is, "I already did all that work, I don't want to redo it." Sometimes, in the valley of your project when you are the deepest down, you may have to trek back and find a different path. This can be a defeating feeling, but if more than one person is pointing out something in your work that is confusing them, don't glaze over it and hope it will all wind up fine in the end. You are just going to frustrate yourself to the detriment of quitting.

It's better to backtrack now and lose two weeks' worth of work than to say, "no it's fine" and get to 95% completion and realize you have a project that isn't worth finishing.

YOUR CREATIVE WORTH IS THE SUM TOTAL OF YOUR WORKS, NOT THIS WORK

If you've made it to The Middle, then you must have liked at least some part of your project enough to keep going. This adventure may have brought you a lot of fulfillment up to this point, and that's a great feeling not every artist can experience through his work. It's a powerful feeling when we are surprised by what we can accomplish, but the same is true when we are stuck. What a horrible sense of self-worth we feel as an artist when we can't go on.

My friend, Ben, is a marathon runner, and an amazing one at that. I've never been able to compete at that level. The most I can do are sprint triathlons and half marathons because God blessed me with what some people call a "nerd's body." I asked him, "out of 26.2 miles, what's the worst mile?" He told me it's mile 16. That's the point at which your body has used up all the available calories and is now eating away at your self-worth as a human being for fuel (That's actual science. No, you can't have a reference). It's a cruel trick your mind plays on you. Your mind says, "How do I get this guy to stop running? I'm tired! I know; I'll attack his ability to parent his child. Hey! I know you are running right now, but do you remember the time you were 30 minutes late to pick up your daughter from school, and she was the last kid there? Pretty low, man. Pretty low."

Our minds are beautiful things, but they will play horrible tricks on us sometimes to get us to stop doing exercises that are physically mentally challenging. What choice does a marathon runner have at defeating those voices? I guess they could stop and just start screaming, "I was at Starbucks and there was a long line! That's why I was late!" but that would be a little weird and not particularly productive. The only two choices a runner has to defeat the voices are to either stop their forward motion (giving their brain more fuel for the failure fire) or walk (run) *forward*.

If you are stuck in The Middle of your project with that feeling of self-loathing, stop reading this and do one 10-minute block of work on your project. And if you can, get up the next day and do 10 more minutes. At this pace, you may not get to the finish line sprinting forward in a beautiful winner's stride, but eventually, after all the other runners have gone home and the course is filled with garbage, you'll see the finish line. And that's all that matters.

CHAPTER 7

Fight or Flight

Stam *(HEBREW)*

"With no purpose, value, or significance."[1]

MY HOPE IS THAT IF YOU'VE READ THIS FAR, you've made it out of The Middle, which means, to continue with the running analogy, you are now in view of the finish line. This is an incredible feeling; but *seeing* the finish line and *touching* the finish line are two completely different things.

One year we took a family vacation to Myrtle Beach. A few of us decided to walk to a pier we saw in the distance.

Our eyes saw the pier, relayed to our brains that the pier was within sight. After our eyes and brains discussed the walk for .2 seconds, they agreed that it was within an easy walking distance, 20 maybe 30 minutes tops. Eyes and brains told legs the plan, and we were off. An hour and a half of walking later, our legs were calling the eyes and brains dirty, dirty liars. Even though we saw the pier, it was still so far off, and the goal didn't seem like it was getting closer no matter how many steps we took. At that point, we turned around and decided it wasn't worth it.

The temptation to turn around and head back is still there as much as it was in the middle. The reasons could be anywhere from:

"This isn't how I thought the project was going to look. This isn't what I set out to make."

or

"It's almost finished, but I hate it."

Famous artists often get famous from the work they never thought was any good to begin with. To the shock of "that guy with the acoustic guitar at every party ever," Liam Gallagher of Oasis hates their song *Wonderwall*, stating, "I can't f***ing stand that f***ing song! Every time I have to sing it I want to gag."[2]

We often look at our work near completion and label it as "Stam" or having no purpose. We don't think it's worth the paper it was created on or the file space it's taking up, and thus enters the temptation to purge it from our lives. Delete.

Michelangelo's Florence Pieta (The Deposition) is considered a masterpiece — a beautiful example of Michelangelo's lifelong commitment to his art. The sculpture, carved from hard marble, depicts Christ after death being pulled from the cross by three other figures.

The way Michelangelo made hard marble look as though the garments on the figures were actually soft fabric that could fall off the sculpture any minute is mind-boggling. The way Christ's body is contorted in a pose that no living being could strike, and the perception of holding the weight of a lifeless, cold body on the other three figures' expressions makes the viewer feel that the portion of marble that resembles Christ could fall over at any minute.

It's stunning.

It's also a personal work from Michelangelo meant for his own tomb. This wasn't a commission. This was meant for no one else except Michelangelo himself and his personal reasons for completing it. He also loathed the work and after eight years of working to complete the piece Michelangelo, in a fit of rage, attempted to destroy the almost completed piece. This wasn't a quick, frustrated hammer taken to the piece either. He lost his senses, destroying the limbs of Christ and Mary Magdalene. The masterpiece was commissioned to be restored, and one can still view the cracks where the limbs were separated from the bodies. In its present form, the piece can be viewed at Museo dell'Opera del Duomo in Florence[3] and Christ is still missing a leg.

REVEAL YOUR WORK

There are many theories as to the reason Michelangelo would destroy a work that took eight years of his life to almost complete. Some say he destroyed it because the pose of Christ's leg was in a shape that suggested an intimate relationship between Christ and The Virgin Mary. Others say he was frustrated with the makeup of the marble not allowing him to finish what he envisioned. Whatever the true reason, I believe if I showed a picture of *Florence Pieta* to a group, the majority would be shocked to learn that the artist attempted its destruction and thought of it as less than a beautiful piece of art.

"Yea, but I'm not Michelangelo and my work really isn't worthy to be seen by anyone. Who cares if I scrap it?"

Says who? Are we really the best judges of our own work?

The temptation to hide or destroy our own work close to completion is a sign that as we near the finish line, fear is manifesting in the thought of completing our project. We don't fear what our work is as an object. We didn't create a bomb that would physically harm anyone. We fear what emotion our work will elicit when we reveal it to the world. We fear opinions and how those opinions will shape our self-worth.

One theory suggested that Michelangelo feared that the Pope would believe the character in the back was actually

Michelangelo himself, which could have been perceived as heresy.

If fear of showing your work is crippling you from finishing your project, it's time to let more people in on what you've been doing in secret.

I've ran one half-marathon in my life. I don't do them anymore. I stick to sprint triathlons because I hate running. The less running I have to do, the better. I remember the day of the half marathon as being unusually hot for mid-April. Around mile 11 or 12, I was dying. Not literally, but the kind of "death" that 16-year-old girls die when Starbucks is closed earlier than they thought. "Literally. Dying. I can't *even* . . ."

At this point, I was running about 15 feet, then walking about 3,456 feet. I was pretty much done with the whole thing when I rounded a corner in downtown Toledo, Ohio. I saw my friend (also named Jason) clapping for me and yelling, "Yea SMITHERS! You got this!" He could see I was struggling; so instead of just offering some encouraging words, he left the street corner and ran *with me*. I can't tell you how that felt when I got out of my own head space and realized someone else was so excited for me to finish that he would even help me get to the finish line. Jason ran with me until about 200 yards away from the finish line. He couldn't physically pick me up and carry me to the finish line, but his encouragement and action did exactly that. When I reached the 200-yard mark, I saw friends and family ready with even more encouragement for me to cross the finish line.

If you've taken the "work in secret" advice, but are mentally exhausted and "Literally, can't even . . ." then it's time to start getting on social media and on the phone with friends to tell them what you've been working on for so long. Don't sweat the trolls. Only the people that are jealous of you or wish ill will toward you will meet you with a negative response. Be honest. Be open to feedback and encouragement:

"Here's a piece I've been working on. I'm almost finished, but I'm not quite there yet. Your thoughts and feedback would be awesome to hear right now."

The encouragement of your Mastermind Jury, friends, and family won't carry you to touch the finish line, but it will give you the mental lift to keep putting one foot in front of the other until you touch that tape.

WHO'S YOUR AUDIENCE?

So who's your audience? Hint. Your audience should be smaller than five people you know really well. End of section.

When I sat down to write this book, I truthfully wasn't sure who my audience was. This being my first non-fiction work, I read a few articles on how to create a synopsis and the same thing kept coming up:

"You need to answer the question: Who's Your Audience?"

In my Trapper Keeper™ labeled "My First Non-Fiction," I put the answer to the question as something horribly generic like this:

"My audience is in the age demographic of 30s-60s who are frustrated with their place in life and unfulfilled by their personal work . . . blah . . . blah . . . blah . . ."

My statement was so generic that I couldn't even fool myself with such a bad summary. I convinced myself that I shouldn't write until I could describe my audience in a clear, concise, sexy elevator pitch. After spending a few weeks wrestling with this, I decided to just write. As I began to write, I realized I was visualizing a conversation with three people specifically — not figureheads.

These are people I know closely. As I typed, it was almost as if they were sitting in front of me, and we were having a conversation over coffee about their personal work and why they've stalled. My writing began to close from a scatter shot "reach as many people as possible" approach to a single thought: If this book could help my friend (insert name), then that's what this is all for.

Author Tim Ferris wrote the first edition of *The 4-Hour Workweek: Escape 9-5, Live Anywhere, and Join the New Rich* back in 2007. Since then the book has sold over 1,350,000 copies, has been translated into over 30 languages, and has spent more years on the *New York Times Best-Seller* list than the amount of years my youngest daughter has been on this earth. The book is groundbreaking and has helped thousands of people shape the way they want to live out the rest of their days on this earth, but one thing stuck out for me more than any other life hacks in the book. It's the first 130 words of the book:

> *"The 4-Hour Workweek was turned down by 26 out of 27 publishers.*
>
> *After it was sold, the president of one potential marketing partner, a large bookseller, e-mailed me historical bestseller statistics to make it clear this wouldn't be a mainstream success.*
>
> *So I did all I knew how to do. I wrote it with two of my closest friends in mind, speaking directly to them and their problems- problems I long had- and I focused on the unusual options that had worked for me around the world.*
>
> *I certainly tried to set conditions for making a sleeper hit possible, but I knew it wasn't likely. I hoped for the best and planned for the worst.*
>
> *May 2, 2007, I receive a call on my cell phone from my editor. "Tim, you hit the list."[4]*

One of the most popular books of the last ten years, enjoyed by millions, was, at its core, written for two people. Only a few artists will enjoy that type of success. That's a feat out of everyone's control. No matter how many books you read on "how to become a famous X" it won't guarantee you that large of an audience. So focus on what you can control in regard to whom your work is for. Ask yourself the following question:

"What friend, co-worker or family member can I complete this work for?"

After you have your answer, your work will have so much more focus. It will also bring a lot of fulfillment in its completion when you can give your work to the individuals who you worked for.

ON MARKETING

We are hopefully at the point in our work where we are 90% confident that we will be finishing. It may not look like what we set out to create. It may have gone better or worse than we had hoped, but either way we are going to finish! It's a great feeling, and it's also a great time to begin telling people what you've been creating. This isn't for the sake of encouragement like we talked about earlier. It's a better reason than that. Now we get to tell people because we feel like our work may add value to their lives. The fact that your project could add value to people's lives may sound kind of arrogant and even make you feel a little uncomfortable, like you just came down from the mountain with a full beard fit for Moses, telling your followers "LO! People of earth! I have communed in the wilderness and worked tirelessly on thine Macbook Air to bring you my latest Dubstep EP! You may now commence with the joyful crying and awkward Dubstep dancing in the streets!" Accept it or not, your project *will* add value to other people's lives. Creative work inspires us, challenges us, makes us nostalgic, makes us think, makes us vulnerable, makes us relate, can have the power to help us forgive, can make us generous, and can usher in change in the world.

One of my favorite TV series in the past few years has been Dave Grohl's *Sonic Highways*. The first season is a beautifully told story of nine different cities in the US and the history of music in those cities. My favorite part about the documentary is that Grohl didn't just interview the most well-known artists in music. He sought to interview the most influential and prolific artists. It was amazing for me to listen to guys who made a punk album 25 years ago, drifted into obscurity, then become the names all the famous people credited as their inspiration to play music. If bands like the Bad Brains or Minor Threat didn't exist, then there may have never been a Nirvana, or Foo Fighters for that matter.

The fact that my work and your work could influence the next big thing blows me away and is frankly way more exciting to me than my own work becoming widely successful. True, you could have both, but I would much rather come to the end of my days with a few people telling me that my work changed them than to have a house of metal awards to show for my work.

If the small chance of adding value to someone's life with your work or the possibility that you could inspire tremendously talented people to take up the same craft fills your tank, then you should get excited about telling others about your work. That is the essential end goal completed by that word that gives some of us the creeps:

"MARKETING"

Marketing, is taking action to promote and sell your products or services. That's it. Telling people about your work. But the word marketing gives us weird visions of greased-up, deceptive businessmen sitting around a smoky room figuring out ways to spin a product in a way that sells the most units, reminiscent of a scene from *Mad Men*.

For this reason alone, people tend to separate themselves from the marketing side of their work and hire people to do it for them. But it's only the professional or semi-professional that has that luxury. The majority of non-professionals don't want to get out there and feel like they are selling themselves, so they either let the project die or figure it out.

Since the goal of this book was never to help you sell X amount of copies of your app or get you X amount of book pre-orders, we are going to focus only on one style of marketing: We are going to shoot to give one format of our finished product away.

GENEROSITY

In my eyes, this is the best type of marketing for the non-professional. You don't have to pay for expensive ads; you don't have to strike up relationships with promoters who are in it for their best interest. You just have to give your project away.

This thought may have rubbed you the wrong way, but here's what I would say to you. You are reading this book because you struggled to finish. Now that you are close to finishing, why not use this moment as a way to share your work generously with the world? This does a few things for us:

1.) It lets the world know you exist, and that you have something to offer without having to worry about the "ask."

We are celebrating the near completion of your work. For this project, we aren't focused on asking people to buy something. We just want them to celebrate our finished project with us. If you were a baker, and you invited a few of us over to try your first completed wedding cake, I would say, "Heck yea! Free cake!" And if it was halfway decent, I would tell my friends about my awesome friend who can create a killer wedding cake (seriously, I will come to your house and eat cake if you want me to, free of charge). But if you just finished your first cake and ask me to buy it, I'm 99% positive I won't buy it. You have no trust built up with me to invest my money in your creation. What if it looks good on the outside, but the batter is raw? I'm more willing to risk food poisoning for free cake though. (How's that cake coming?)

2.) People criticize free stuff a lot less.

Well, most people. There are still going to be the occasional, entitled jerks that complain when the free wifi is slow or that the free samples of Go-Gurt in the grocery store are only strawberry flavored, but the majority of people will be much more appreciative that you've shared your work with them and will offer you a more softened critique.

3.) You convert an audience to fans.

I mentioned the author and CEO of Breather, Julien Smith, earlier in this book. Julien gave away his book *The Flinch* for a time, and was generous with freely offering me advice. He's one of the reasons this book exists. His generosity made me a fan for life. When Julien releases a product, you can bet I'll be one of the first to check it out and tell others about it. Giving generously of our work is very much an intangible investment. We can't calculate what the return could potentially be by giving a stranger some free art prints, but I can promise you this: there is nothing lost in being a generous person.

METHODS OF GENEROSITY

Setting up ways to be generous that coincide with the completion of your project shouldn't feel like a chore. There are plenty of ways to make it fun. My friend and very talented Canadian artist, Ruth Oosterman, who created the UNFINISHED bird on the cover, creates these fantastic paintings with her daughter. She allows her daughter to paint whatever she wants, and then Ruth comes in after and translates her daughter's brushstrokes into the figures she sees within it. The results are stunning. Ruth encourages this act with other parents by running contests for parents and their children where the parents are encouraged to submit a painting they did with their children. The winners typically get an original painting by Ruth and her daughter, or a signed print. I did this with my daughter, and it was so much fun.

She added value to my relationship with my older daughter through her art.

Some projects are easy to give away and don't necessarily have to be a big event: copies of music, digital downloads, prints of your original art. They are inexhaustible resources so give them away like crazy. Leave them at your local coffee shop; give them to your waitress or a random stranger on the street.

My friend, Micah, created a dice app entitled, *Dice & Dragons* for players of tabletop games. It's free to download and offers a ton of options to make dice rolling addition easy. The free version of the app has now been downloaded more than 142,000 times. The users who would like more of an in-depth experience can download a paid portion of the app. Micah created a lot of fans and converted a portion of them into paid users by first giving his product away. What Micah doesn't say is that he's put at least 120 hours into the free portion of the app. Micah will never get rich off of this app. It's not why he does it. He knows his app adds value (less math, more time enjoying the game) and wants as many people to have the same experience he has had with *Dice & Dragons*.

Along with the app being nominated for an "eNie" award, Micah tells a great story of a mom that emailed him to say "thanks" because her autistic son was going to have to quit playing D&D with his friends. He slowed down the game so badly because of his math skills. The quick calculations in Micah's app made it possible for this woman's son to play with his friends without feeling like an outcast.

If you are a musical artist, whatever you think about Spotify and other digital music streaming services, there's one thing that you can't debate: it's made artists who would normally live in obscurity widely popular. Sean Parker, creator of Napster, has one of the most followed playlists on Spotify. One day, back in 2013, he added a fairly unknown artist to his playlist that is now followed by more than 800,000 people. That artist was Lorde, and after 2013, there wasn't a person on the planet that wasn't familiar with her song *Royals*. Lorde made her music free to listeners through Spotify, and in return, her act of generosity was a catalyst to her winning two Grammys in 2014 for Song of the Year and Best Pop Solo Performance[5].

Generosity always wins.

Jason Smithers

CHAPTER 8

It's *Mine*

Suaimhneas Croi *(IRISH)*

"A bursting happiness and peace encountered after a task has been finished and there is nothing left to be done."[1]

THE EXPERT GATEKEEPER

REVEALING WHAT YOU'VE BEEN WORKING on this whole time might have made you feel one of two things. It either gets you excited or makes you want to run to the nearest trash can and rid yourself of today's diet of a Capri Sun and Hot Pockets (That only goes for those in college or who have kids under the age of 10). The excitement is predicated on the pride you feel for what you have accomplished and knowing that others may feel the same feelings you had while working. The queasy stomach is because you decided Hot Pockets and Capri Sun wasn't a good idea in the first place OR because the thought of people judging your work makes you want to crawl into a hole.

There's also a third feeling that's a little harder to observe. It's the feeling of confidence in your work. But I don't mean the good kind of confidence; I mean the kind that tells you that you *know* your work is BAD. "I'm confident this work is terrible."

There's a folder on my computer labeled "Songwriting." These are songs I wrote or co-wrote from 2012 to present. There are over 100 songs that I will never allow to see the light of day. Why? Because I have confidence from my years of songwriting that these are objectively bad songs. When I say they are objectively bad, I mean that I have held these songs up to other songs I've deemed to be benchmarks for good songs, and they didn't pass. The rhyming schemes are bad; the lyrics are stale; it sounds like a rip-off of another song, etc.

My fear is there are some of you, like me, that have been doing your craft for so long that you know the ins and outs of it, so much so that your friends find you a little insufferable to be around when talking about it. I once asked some close friends for feedback on what I could work on in my personality, and one friend told me he didn't feel like he could share the music he loved with me because I would probably just rip it apart. Being an expert gatekeeper may have brought you to the point where you think you know your own craft so well that you won't let anything you deem bad work to see the light of day. You may have also been such a vocal critic of other's work in person or on social media that releasing your project to the world means you have to "put your money where your mouth is" and live up to a higher standard than the work you've criticized.

INVISIBLE VS. VULNERABLE

There's a feeling that you get that's a bit hard to describe once the last word is written down, the last test is run on the app, and the code flies. The Irish call the positive side of completion "Suaimhneas Croi." But completion can also come with a feeling of extreme excitement, mixed with times of fear, like the care and paranoia a mother feels as her child gets on the school bus for the first time. More times than I can count, I've settled in for a good night's sleep only to throw open my eyelids and wonder if I chose the right font for my children's book, or if the right person was doing backup vocals on a song we just cut. I mean, it makes sense... think of all the kids that could turn to a life of drugs and hard crime if I chose the wrong font, right??

It's in the caring for our work that helps it be the best project possible — or it can absolutely smother the life out of it. These are the moments that cause us to do desperate things, such as Michelangelo taking a hammer to a masterpiece.

*Note to reader: I get to self-publish this book. There are many benefits to going the traditional route, but one disadvantage would be that the publisher probably wouldn't let me use THREE *Lord of the Rings*/Tolkien analogies. Here goes the third:

If you've never been a fan of *The Lord of the Rings*, then congratulations, you were probably cool in high school and didn't have to talk to girls primarily on AOL Instant Messenger because the thought of a phone call made you pee your pants. I'll quickly explain the premise. There's a powerful ring that a bad guy wants, but the good guys want to keep this ring from him. The bad guy will stop at nothing to get the ring back, and the good guys realize that the only way to stop the bad guy is to destroy the ring in a volcano really, really far away. A tiny person named Frodo speaks up and says, "I'll do it." His adventure progresses with many challenges. The ring gives him the supernatural power to be invisible, but it is also an extreme burden for him to carry. He is tired and ready to be finished with this adventure.

At the end of this epic tale, after Frodo has spent the entire adventure trying to get The Ring of Power to Mt. Doom to destroy it, there's a conflicting moment. This whole journey has led up to this one task. All he has to do is drop the ring into the fires of Mt. Doom and he defeats the evil Sauron. But the ring has become a part of him. As much pain as the ring has caused him, it has also become familiar. Comforting. After much goading from his traveling companion, Samwise, to "Throw it in the fire!" he finally turns from the fires and says, "No; it's *mine*."

That line gets me every time. Why wouldn't he just send it away? What caused him to hold on to it? My theory is that he found comfort in the power the ring gave him to be invisible. He didn't have to face the world; he could hide away in a dark place. Sure, the dark places had their own discomforts, but maybe it was better than living in a harsh world where Trolls, Giant Spiders, and Orcs were always hunting you.

I think that's why we hold onto our personal projects when we finish. Why not just enjoy it for ourselves? Why release our work into the real world where it will be picked apart, torn to shreds, and criticized for every imperfection? That's why we hold on to our work. After all, **being invisible is much better than being vulnerable.**

I had a really difficult time with the thought of our older daughter starting kindergarten. Kids are mean, and she's very sensitive. Why subject her to the world? Why not just hide her away and not expose her to what oftentimes can be a cruel world? I found the answer one day when my daughter decided to make a nice thank-you card for our waitress. When Maci gave the waitress the card, the waitress's mood instantly changed. Maci was a blessing in her day. That's when I realized that I would be selfish to keep this awesome little person to myself. She was made to make the world better, and she does. When she goes to school, the majority of the kids perk up and yell, "HI MACI!" Her presence adds value in their lives.

Your work is your child. It's young, vulnerable, and the world can break it. But if this is where the thoughts about your work stop, you are dead wrong. Your work has the ability to heal, to delight, to connect, to speak truth, to insight incidences. Releasing your work to the world doesn't guarantee it won't be torn to shreds and in turn, tear you apart, but not releasing it 100% guarantees no one will be positively affected.

It's time to put that little kid on the school bus.

CHAPTER 9

A Gift

Raison D'Etre *(FRENCH)*

*"The most important reason or purpose for someone
or something's existence."[1]*

WILLIAM WAS A HARD-WORKING HUSBAND and
father to six children. In the mid 2000s, William was working
three jobs just to get his family through these very difficult
times. His family lost their home, and by his words had
become "working poor." This journey, and the stress of
feeding and housing a family of eight, could have crushed just
about any man, but William searched for the opportunity to
learn from the situation. He took stock of the small moments
in life, and if he had to clean toilets for a living, then he would
be the best toilet cleaner he could.

"Contentment, assuredly, has nothing to do with situation and circumstance. "Rags to riches" is truly an internal journey, not an external one," he once said in an article with The Huffington Post.

You see, William also loved to write and during this difficult time in life, he decided to turn what he'd learned about trials in life into a story for his children. A gift. I imagine he carved out precious time in his extremely busy days because a gift to his loved ones mattered more than taking 15 minutes for himself.

> *"The Shack, a work of 'true' fiction (think, parable), I wrote as a Christmas gift at a time when there was little else to give. I made 15 copies at Office Depot, delivered them to family and friends, and went back to work. In retrospect, I am grateful that I truly had no real idea of what I had done, that everything that matters to me was in place before I wrote this story and that the first fifteen copies did all that I ever wanted this novel to do."*[2]

Some friends helped William set up a publishing company, and the rest is truly literary history. *The Shack* has gone on to sell more than 18 Million copies. **18 Million**! That's unreal.

Without knowing William Young's back story, my guess is that the average reader or inspiring author picked up *The Shack* and assumed Young was just another gifted author who was hustling to "make it big."

A cliché.

Instead, his story makes it a much more beautiful story and to me, the ideal model for this book:

• Young was a non-professional creator.

• He carved out the time to work on his craft to completion.

• His motive was purely to give a gift.

If William's story ended before the wild success of the book, it would still be an ideal story. If I were to imagine what I would want the result of this book to be, it would be to have a handful of people tell me that it helped them:

• Put the notion of 'getting famous' in the trash.

• Do the hard work and carve out time to finish projects in their busy lives.

• Have someone in mind for whom they are creating their work.

• Give their work as a gift to those people

There is no "and get famous" bullet point.

Young had his head on straight before the fame cycle got a hold of _The Shack_. I've never met Young, but I had the opportunity to hear him speak at a conference and there was no arrogance or ego. Young has no sense of entitlement because of his success, and his humility and "down-to-earthness" are genuine. Fame didn't change Young, but his work changed millions of lives. Young writes further in his Huffington Post article:

> *"Largely through the kindness, support and grace of others, this little gift was delivered to the world and it became a force for transformation and conversation in the global community, largely, I suspect, an expression of God's sense of humor and affection. Eighteen million copies, and 41 languages later, we all still shake our heads and laugh. This is not the story of reward for a life well lived; anyone who knows me understand this. This is an expression of the grace of a God who is good all the time and involved in the details of our lives, in the ordinary and routine."*

You and your work have a "raison d'être." A purpose in existence. And that purpose is found in being gifted to be a gift.

PULL BACK THE CURTAINS

At this point you are one of three types of people:

1. You've used this book as a guide coinciding with your project and are reading this section as you finish.

2. You read the book straight through and (hopefully) it's inspired you to get to work

3. You are my mom. (Hi, again, Mom!)

If you've completed your project or you are my mom, read on. If you haven't started, it's time. If you've finished, then I'm so excited for you! I would love to hear about your story and your project! Email me at Jason@unfinished.life.

This moment is a beautiful time to be proud of the work you've finished. You completed something only you could complete. A thought turned into a plan. You gave your project a skeleton, muscles, and tendons. You gave it emotion and feelings that others can now connect to. You brought it to life. You made something from literally nothing.

As this gift is released to the people you want to gift it to — whether friends, family, or a larger audience — take a moment to journal your ups and downs of the process. You'll have unique observations to share with others that may ask, "How did you do it?"

My hope is that you pull back the curtain for others that want to do what you do. My friend, Ruth Oosterman, whom I mentioned in a previous chapter, posts time-lapse videos of the creation process of her canvas collaborations with her daughter. There is no part of her method she doesn't openly share with the world.

You've been gifted to be a gift not only with the product of your hard work, but also with your knowledge of how to get to "Finished." Massive Open Online Courses or MOOCs (Like Coursera or Udemy), have exploded over the past few years because it makes learning a craft so accessible.

Give away your secrets. Throw up a quick three to four-minute video on YouTube of how you got to "finished."

Teach the next generation of artists your craft and gift because you have been gifted.

CONCLUSION

The Unfinished Life

Gesamtkunstwerk (GERMAN)

"Complete work, an entire body of work. Coined by Wagner."[1]

MADE FOR THE JOURNEY

I PREVIOUSLY MENTIONED THE KICKSTARTER that many amazing people donated to, allowing a few very close friends and me to release an EP before my wife and I moved away from our hometown; but I never mentioned what happened after it was finished. After the songs were recorded, mixed, mastered, and printed, it was time to ship the EP out. I already had my victory. I already held the finished product in my hand. This part wasn't a big deal. All I had to do was put the CDs in some type of mailer and send out 100+ CDs to the backers of this Kickstarter. I thought an envelope with a thank-you-card signed by the artists involved would be a nice touch and would suffice in shipping. So I spent my time in the post office line of purgatory, shipped the CDs, and didn't think about it for the rest of the week. My part was done. All that was left was for the backers to listen and make their own decisions if what we did was good or bad, right?

WRONG.

I was with my wife and friends having a great time at Universal Studios when the first few emails and Facebook messages started coming in.

"Hey, my CD doesn't work. It looks like it got messed up somehow."

"There's a warp in the CD, and it doesn't seem to want to play for me."

"I think the heat in Florida may have messed my CD up."

You know that feeling when you go from happy to panic very quickly? When your body heat rises 20 degrees above normal and your hands start sweating?

That was me.

What I would later find out is that you can't just put a CD in the regular mail with the rest of the Happy Birthday cards to your nephews and nieces. The envelopes go through some hefty rollers that make sure the envelopes aren't too big. My envelopes were just thick enough to go through the rollers, but not thin enough to avoid the crushing weight of the oversized pizza rollers of death.

Every single CD I sent out was ruined. All of them became a useless piece of plastic. This was never a project we were thinking of making any bigger than inside the circle of our supporters, so I only ordered enough CDs for the backers. I lost a lot of sleep because the generous people that gave us their hard-earned money had essentially received a glorified coaster for their support. I had to rush ship another order of CDs and paid for it not only in the monetary sense, but it extinguished the feelings of accomplishment I had when I first opened the case of CDs.

If you were to ask me in that moment of panic in the middle of Universal Studios if I wanted to do another music project, I'm pretty sure I would have grabbed a Harry Potter wand from the gift shop and cast a balding curse on you.

"HAIROUS FALLOUTOUS!!"

I shipped the new CDs out and really didn't want to think about doing another music project any time soon. After all, at least I finished, right?

Your finished work may have ended up like my CD catastrophe, or it may have gone even better than you would have hoped. In both instances, regardless of what you hoped for, you are not finished. My hope is that through this book, I awoke a confidence in you that you can complete projects. You were made to create continuously. You wouldn't be reading this book if you didn't have the desire in your gut to create.

That desire to create is a thread that aches to weave through the ups and downs in life. It wants you to create in the tough times because it knows the honest work you create will connect with someone in the same circumstances. It wants you to create when life is full of laughs in the company of friends and family, so that others can know that life can be good and worth living. It wants you to create in the final stages of life, because the thread knows it will need to leave you soon and pick up a path through someone else's story.

Your work, or your thread, will carry past your lifetime. It may not be in obvious ways. People may never gaze for hours at your art in a museum and speculate if you were a crazed genius or a prolific force of your time. The thread in your work that others will pick up may be as simple as, "If they can finish, so can I." It may be a brush stroke that makes someone's head tilt and becomes a catalyst for a whole new style. You will never know your full impact during this lifetime — and that's ok.

I'm finishing this book in hopes that I have not only guided you to completion of a project, but that I have also reignited a lifelong love affair within you to continuously add value to the world. Work hard in the process; find opportunities to learn from the disasters and imperfections in your completed projects. They are catalysts for your next work to be better. Rethink your approaches and try something new the next time around.

Truthfully, I'm writing this as I near the final minutes of a yearlong process in creating this book during a really difficult time in my life. This is extremely hard to finish. I'm the first runner on the relay team that is in the final seconds of the sprint and I'm reaching to pass the baton off to you.

As you grab the baton, I'm gulping air down, breathing in the feeling of my part in this race being completed. As my lungs fill, my eyes are on you to finish well. Run your part of the race until the last second when that baton leaves your hand and passes to another. We are doing this together. It does us no good as a team to hold the baton and sit waiting for inspiration.

After the stadium is empty, you and I will rest and prepare to start again, because our work on this earth is and will always be... Unfinished.

Acknowledgements

Special Thanks:

To my Jessica Smithers who patiently and thoughtfully read through every iteration of this book. Thank you for believing in this project and helping to see it through. I love you!

To Barbara Smithers, Deborah Becton, Joshua White, Jamie Deighton and Micah Sawyer for taking time to provide suggestions, line edits, and copy edits on my early drafts. I'm humbled to have friends and family that would take their time to do this for me. You all are amazing!

Final Manuscript Line and Copy Edits: Marjorie Poff

Cover Art: Ruth Oosterman

Cover Design and Type: Amanda Tuttle

Bibliography

Introduction

1.Torschlusspanik. (n.d.). Retrieved January 6, 2016, from
https://en.wiktionary.org/wiki/Torschlusspanik

2. Graham, S. (2005, August 8). Brain Region Tied to Regret Identified.
Retrieved January 6, 2016, from
http://www.scientificamerican.com/article/brain-region-tied-to-regr/

Chapter 1

1. Moore, C. (2004). In other words: A language lover's guide to the most
intriguing words around the world. New York: Walker Pub.

2. Money, M. (2010, September 8). Personal Finance Basics: Negative Events
Will Happen To You. Plan Ahead With Insurance And An Emergency Fund.
Retrieved January 6, 2016, from http://www.smartonmoney.com/personal-
finance-basics-negative-events-will-happen-to-you-plan-ahead-with-
insurance-and-an-emergency-fund/

3. Acuff, J. (2011). Quitter: Closing the gap between your day job & your
dream job. Brentwood, TN: Lampo Press, The Lampo Group.

Chapter 2

1. Ikigai (Japanese). (2012, November 13). Retrieved January 6, 2016, from
http://betterthanenglish.com/ikigai-japanese/

2. Murphy, M. (2011). Hard goals: The secrets to getting from where you are
to where you want to be. New York: McGraw-Hill.

Chapter 3

1. Nubie Yom (Swahili). (2013, August 9). Retrieved January 6, 2016, from
http://betterthanenglish.com/nubie-yom-swahili/

2. Horowitz, A. (2011, April 25). 15 People Who Were Fired Before They Became Filthy Rich. Retrieved January 6, 2016, from http://www.businessinsider.com/15-people-who-were-fired-before-they-became-filthy-rich-2011-4?op=1

3. Why Squinting Helps You See Better. (2013, November 13). Retrieved January 6, 2016, from http://www.todayifoundout.com/index.php/2013/11/squinting-helps-see-better/

Chapter 4

1. (2015, November 19). Retrieved January 6, 2016, from https://en.wikipedia.org/wiki/Tsundoku

2. Lamott, A. (n.d.). Bird by bird: Some instructions on writing and life.

3. Zerubavel, E. (1999). The clockwork muse: A practical guide to writing theses, dissertations, and books. Cambridge, Mass.: Harvard University Press.

4. (2015, September 30). Retrieved January 6, 2016, from https://en.wikipedia.org/wiki/Ultraman_(endurance_challenge)

5. The Brain's Dopamine Neurotransmitter. (n.d.). Retrieved January 6, 2016, from http://www.psychologistworld.com/biological/neurotransmitters/dopamine.php

6. Zerubavel, E. (1999). The clockwork muse: A practical guide to writing theses, dissertations, and books. Cambridge, Mass.: Harvard University Press.

Chapter 5

1. (2015, October 24). Retrieved January 6, 2016, from https://en.wikipedia.org/wiki/Sprezzatura

2. McKeown, G. (2014). Essentialism: The disciplined pursuit of less. Crown Business.

3. Transcript of "Keep your goals to yourself" (2010, September 1). Retrieved January 6, 2016, from https://www.ted.com/talks/derek_sivers_keep_your_goals_to_yourself/transcript?language=en

Chapter 6
1. Oltuski, R. (2012, August 13). 11 More Wonderful Words With No English Equivalent. Retrieved January 8, 2016, from http://mentalfloss.com/article/31458/11-more-wonderful-words-no-english-equivalent

2. Tolkien, J. (1966). The hobbit, or, There and back again,. Boston: Houghton Mifflin.

3. (2015, July 11). Retrieved January 8, 2016, from https://en.wikipedia.org/wiki/The_Eagle_and_Child

Chapter 7
1. Stam (Hebrew). (2012, May 27). Retrieved January 8, 2016, from http://betterthanenglish.com/stam-hebrew/

2. Van Rheenen, E. (2015, October 9). 10 Artists Who Hated Their Biggest Hit. Retrieved January 8, 2016, from http://mentalfloss.com/article/51906/10-artists-who-hated-their-biggest-hit

3. (2015, October 3). Retrieved January 8, 2016, from https://en.wikipedia.org/wiki/The_Deposition_(Michelangelo)

4. Ferriss, T. (2007). *The 4-hour workweek: Escape 9-5, live anywhere, and join the new rich*. New York: Crown.

5. Bertoni, S. (2013, November 26). How Spotify Made Lorde A Pop Superstar. Retrieved January 8, 2016, from http://www.forbes.com/sites/stevenbertoni/2013/11/26/how-spotify-made-lorde-a-pop-superstar/

Chapter 8

1. Suaimhneas croi (Irish). (2011, December 8). Retrieved January 8, 2016, from http://betterthanenglish.com/suaimhneas-croi-irish/

Chapter 9

1. "raison dêtre." The Oxford Pocket Dictionary of Current English. 2009. (2009). Raison dêtre. Retrieved January 8, 2016, from http://www.encyclopedia.com/doc/1O999-raisondetre.html

2. Young, W. (2012, November 5). 'The Shack': How a Story for My Children Became a New York Times Best Seller. Retrieved January 8, 2016, from http://www.huffingtonpost.com/wm-paul-young/the-shack-how-a-story-for-my-children-became-a-new-york-times-best-seller_b_2124683.html

Conclusion

1. Gesamtkunstwerk (German). (2011, August 2). Retrieved January 8, 2016, from http://betterthanenglish.com/gesamtkunstwerk-german/#comments

30-Day Buffet

Here are a few ideas for a 30 Day Buffet of experiences :

Day One: Draw a nonsense creature, something that a reasonable person couldn't say what it looks like ☐

Day Two: Write lyrics to a song; don't worry about structure ☐

Day Three: Try Yoga for 30 minutes ☐

Day Four: Buy an instrument ☐

Day Five: Write a one-page story ☐

Day Six: Take 30 photographs and post to Instagram with the hashtag #30picturesaday ☐

Day Seven: Sign up for free Crossfit session ☐

Day Eight: Sign up for Codeacademy.com ☐

Day Nine: Buy three albums outside of your normal genres ☐

Day Ten: Spend an hour learning to act ☐

Day Eleven: Write a poem ☐

Day Twelve: Watch a random documentary ☐

Day Thirteen: Join Meetup.com and join a group ☐

Day Fourteen: Listen to a Tim Ferris Show Podc

30-Day Buffet (continued)

Day Fifteen: Take a business course on Udemy.com ☐

Day Sixteen: Check out one hobby book at the Library ☐

Day Seventeen: Signup for VolunteerMatch.org ☐

Day Eighteen: Watch three videos on Ted.com ☐

Day Nineteen: Ask an Author for a 10min conversation ☐

Day Twenty: Sign up for a class at an Art Museum ☐

Day Twenty-One: Free write for 30 minutes ☐

Day Twenty-Two: Google "Nobody Tells This To Beginners" ☐

Day Twenty-Three: Watch '20,000 Days on Earth' ☐

Day Twenty-Four: Film a five minute tutorial video on something you enjoy doing and upload to Youtube ☐

Day Twenty-Five: Google 'Newspaper Blackout Poetry' and try doing your own ☐

Day Twenty-Six: Ask a friend to borrow one of their instruments and learn to play it for 30 minutes ☐

Day Twenty-Seven: Audition for a part in a play at your local theater ☐

30-Day Buffet (continued)

Day Twenty-Eight: Buy Seth Godin's book Purple Cow and read the first two chapters ☐

Day Twenty-Nine: Spend thirty minutes writing a dialog scene between two people ☐

Day Thirty: Reflect back on this 30 day exercise and what you've learned about yourself. Journal your revelations ☐

30-Day Buffet (Blank Template)

Here you can create your own 30-Day Buffet based off of the ideas in the previous example.

Day One:_____ ☐

Day Two:_____ ☐

Day Three:_____ ☐

Day Four:_____ ☐

Day Five: _____ ☐

Day Six: _____ ☐

Day Seven:_____ ☐

Day Eight:_____ ☐

Day Nine: _____ ☐

Day Ten: _____ ☐

Day Eleven:_____ ☐

Day Twelve:_____ ☐

Day Thirteen:_____ ☐

Day Fourteen:_____ ☐

30-Day Buffet (Blank Template Continued)

Day Fifteen:_____ □

Day Sixteen:_____ □

Day Seventeen:_____ □

Day Eighteen:_____ □

Day Nineteen: _____ □

Day Twenty: _____ □

Day Twenty-One:_____ □

Day Twenty-Two:_____ □

Day Twenty-Three:_____ □

Day Twenty-Four: _____ □

Day Twenty-Five:_____ □

Day Twenty-Six:_____ □

Day Twenty-Seven:_____ □

Day Twenty-Eight:_____ □

Day Twenty-Nine:_____ □

Day Thirty:_____ □

ABOUT THE AUTHOR

Jason Smithers (@Jasondsmithers) is a husband/father foremost then writer, music producer and photographer.

To start a conversation, email Jason: Jason@unfinished.life